FEAR LESS

ALSO BY TRACY K. SMITH

POETRY COLLECTIONS

Such Color: New and Selected Poems

Wade in the Water

Life on Mars

Duende

The Body's Question

MEMOIRS

Ordinary Light

To Free the Captives: A Plea for the American Soul

CO-TRANSLATED WITH CHANGTAI BI

My Name Will Grow Wide Like a Tree: Selected Poems of Yi Lei

COEDITED WITH JOHN FREEMAN

There's a Revolution Outside, My Love: Letters from a Crisis

NORTON
SHORTS

FEAR LESS

Poetry in Perilous Times

TRACY K. SMITH

W. W. NORTON & COMPANY
Independent Publishers Since 1923

Copyright © 2025 by Tracy K. Smith

All rights reserved
Printed in the United States of America
First Edition

For information about permission to reproduce selections from this book, write to Permissions, W. W. Norton & Company, Inc., 500 Fifth Avenue, New York, NY 10110

For information about special discounts for bulk purchases, please contact W. W. Norton Special Sales at specialsales@wwnorton.com or 800-233-4830

Manufacturing by Lakeside Book Company
Production manager: Delaney Adams

Since this page cannot legibly accommodate all the copyright notices, pages 171–73 constitute an extension of the copyright page.

ISBN: 978-1-324-05098-8

W. W. Norton & Company, Inc.
500 Fifth Avenue, New York, NY 10110
www.wwnorton.com

W. W. Norton & Company Ltd.
15 Carlisle Street, London W1D 3BS

10 9 8 7 6 5 4 3 2

for Raf

CONTENTS

FEAR LESS:
A Poem Is a Tool for Careful Listening — 1

FALLING AWAKE:
Poetry and the Work of the Unconscious — 15

ANY SMALL THING CAN SAVE YOU:
On Grief and Accountability — 50

WHO ARE YOU?:
On Strangers and Others — 81

FEATS OF CONSCIOUSNESS:
Poetry Is a Redeeming Act — 115

BE YE NOT AFRAID:
A Brief Guide to What Poems Are and
How They Do What They Do — 120

ACKNOWLEDGMENTS — 152

APPENDIX OF POETS — 155

NOTES — 167

CREDITS — 171

INDEX — 174

FEAR LESS

FEAR LESS
A Poem Is a Tool for Careful Listening

———

Throughout my reading life, poems have greeted me with what feels like urgent compassion. When I'm lost or afraid, the speakers of poems assure me that my feelings are nothing to hide from or deny—indeed, that vulnerability, uncertainty, and even desperation are not only signs of life, but tools for moving forward toward courage, hope, and purpose. When I'm confident in my convictions, poems alert me to complexities I've failed or been unwilling to regard. And like the best of friends, somehow the poems I've loved for years manage to keep evolving, meeting me where I am and then—how do they do it?—leading me still further along toward what will startle, console, and even change me. I shouldn't be surprised. Our very selves from day to day are the result of where we've been, what we've seen, how we've hurt and healed, and what we are on the threshold even now of discovering. We never cease in our becoming. Neither does this art form, this confidant, this tool designed to remind us how it feels and why it matters to love, to remember, to ache, to fear, to be astonished by what our minds can make and what our spirits can withstand.

Poems exist in language, but their intention is to travel beyond the system of words and logic into systems of sound, sensation, memory, imagination, emotion, knowledge, and ultimately into insight. If you hold this view in mind—that poems *use* words but are not *about* words, the same way cars use fuel or electricity but are *about* something much more far-reaching—then you can feel confident that whoever you are and whatever you care about, you are already perfectly equipped to experience and even to claim a relationship to the art form.

The intention of a poem—like a car, come to think of it—is to take you someplace. Into someone's life or their psyche: their sense of wish or hope, revelation or regret. A stranger approaches, whispers into your ear—*Hey, let me tell you what it was like*—and proceeds to take you far beyond your known self and your intrinsic view of the world. In so doing they might also remind you of something new (or long forgotten) about who you are or who you once were. Obviously, it's not the body that journeys—though sometimes the vivid details in a poem can make you feel that way. No, a poem invites its various forms of departure via conscious perception: your ability to "see" an image or "hear" a sound as it appears; introspection: your ability to look inward and tap into your own feelings, memories, and emotions; and your powers of imagination, which can be sent out far beyond the material self to draw upon what you know and also upon what you can gather or intuit.

I was drawn to poetry because I felt small. I was nineteen, a college sophomore away from home for the first time in a place where everyone seemed better at all the things my teachers and parents had always praised in me. In my insecurity, reading poems allowed me to take notice of things I too often overlooked. Poems slowed down time so that I could observe, reflect, ask, and even muster the urge to assert what I kept bottled up. And so I feel inclined to believe that wherever else it leads, the journey of a poem—every poem—also leads invariably to you, Reader.

I wish I could say to everyone who lives with the fear of poetry: You don't always have to understand it. You can let it nudge you, let it cause something to stir. The sounds of words gliding along next to one another. The glimpse of an image—a face, a body taking flight. Rain hammering down in the night. The difference between the droplets hitting houses and those landing in trees. A blanket of sound covering everything it sees.

What I mean is, I don't always understand the poems I admire. Sometimes poems operate by a logic that eludes me, the way dreams often do. Sometimes, like a conversation with a wonderful stranger, a poem speaks to me in words I know, while leading me down paths that are startling and unfamiliar. Some poems seem to carry me away from my usual thoughts, my usual self, which can feel like a gift. How often do we feel overwhelmed in the lives we know? How often does the world as we have come to recognize it—the world as we have been taught to see it—fill us with fright?

Far from something to fear, I'd say that poetry is an art form that allows us to redefine our relationship to fear by stepping in close to the facets of the world that we don't like, or don't understand. Often enough, these are the same things. Often enough, it is the illusion of extraordinary distance, blurring out details and shrouding motives in shadow, that makes us fearsome to one another. Not always, of course, but often enough. It's not always possible to test out such a theory in life, but poems are built to bridge distances of all kinds: between people and events separated from one another by time, geography, temperament, and belief. A poem can even traverse the distance between the living and the dead.

The first tools were stone, we've been told. Heavy blunt round stones that could be dropped or pounded down upon a thing until it splintered or split or yielded its treasure. Sharp stones like blades that could cut or wedge, that could pierce flesh or convince another thing to part. This is what we've been told. But wasn't song a tool? And story, too? The kiss would have predated the hammerstone or the anvil stone, I am certain. Tools of gift, of need, of intention, of imagination. Tools—let's call them what they rightly are: technologies—of mind and spirit.

If you are reading these pages because you love poetry, then I would like to convince you that poems, if you allow them to, can help you to love every other thing in the world around you. Imagine that. Imagine what it would mean to allow a poem, which can empower you beyond the apprehension of threat, to move you closer and closer to that which you do not love, allowing you to observe, imagine and feel your way past indifference or suspicion and toward recognition. Let's leave it there for the time being, because recognition is the threshold for a great deal more.

And if you have read thus far because poetry is something that you do not as of yet love, something that has made you feel confused or self-conscious or inadequate, then my wish is to convince you that the opposite of love is not hatred or rancor but fear, and to help clear that impediment from this and perhaps other contexts in your life. I want to do this not for but with you, because you and I are not alone. We dwell together in a world riddled with reasons for despair. A world brimming, too, with forms of beauty that fill us with awe, joy, wonder. Fear on the one hand, and something like love on the other.

IN 2017, I WAS appointed Poet Laureate of the United States by Librarian of Congress Dr. Carla Hayden. The opportunity to act as an ambassador between the art form I practice and the nation to which I belong came at a delicate time in American history. Maybe all times are delicate, but by 2017 we'd come to find ourselves in a climate of language—I'd call it a national vocabulary—grounded in fear, derision, and the notion of an intractably divided nation. The guardrails of courtesy were gone, and the limits of shame—or was it shamelessness?—had been set further out than almost ever before. Or so it felt. At the same time, so much talk—on podcasts and radio and TV—added unceasing fodder to the rumor that unless we lived in the same place and prayed to the same deity and voted the same way, we in this country had nothing whatsoever to say to one another. It was a bruise on the collective imagination, a threat to the sense of hope and possibility.

But I thought about the poems my students and I discussed with one another each week. The near-holy hush in the room as we read aloud from the work of poets like Elizabeth Bishop, Gwendolyn Brooks, Robert Hayden, and contemporaries Claudia Rankine, Natalie Diaz, Patrick Rosal, and others. It wasn't only delight that held us in such a state; it was the desire to listen at the widest possible angle, and the proper tilt of the imagination, in order to catch what the voice on the page was asking us to hear, feel, see, remember, and recognize. At such a pitch of attention—which is not passive but active—so much of your energy is invested in maintaining the signal that another voice is transmitting. You may have questions. Doubts, eventually, too. But in good listeners, those things emerge as the result of having first submitted fully to the voice and the imagination before you. Considered in this way, the audience of a poem is undertaking something like a trust-fall. *Come what may*, we are ideally willing to say to the poem, *I'm here, I'm in your hands.*

This isn't, generally speaking, the mode in which we dwell. It's not the way we go about gathering the information that informs so many of our small and large decisions. It's certainly not the way we tend to take in another person's opinion about sports or parenting or politics, where our listening is tense as we await the chance to launch our own argument or defense. Almost daily during the long and histrionic news cycle leading up to the 2016 election, I had found myself thinking, *Poetry wouldn't allow us to behave this way.* I just knew that poetry, a kind of mother to so many, would find a way to jostle us out of our rote engagement with one another. Poetry would insist that our listening be permitted to lead us, even briefly, out of our rigid stances, our staunchest habits. Already I could hear Mother Poetry saying: *Come. Sit. Calm yourselves and attend more generously to one another.* So when the opportunity arose to create a national poetry project with the Library of Congress, I determined to push back against the inescapable narrative of America as a divided nation— the narrative that says people in the rural heartland have next to nothing in common with those of us in urban centers, and that differences of race, class, religion, and citizenship status had sawed us into a puzzle that would never be pieced back together.

I also wanted to test out my own theory that Americans of all backgrounds might have something quietly urgent and humanizing to offer to one another, if only we could turn down the volume on all the many sources seeking to sell us on the notion of an unmendable divide—to hook us on a product, which is strife. In order to get to community, we have to go quiet, slow down, allow ourselves to be both vulnerable and brave, and approach one another with an idea as simple as, *I'm me, you're you, we are not the same, and yet perhaps we can feel safe here together talking about something as simple as a poem*, which encourages the notion that your life must be as important to you as mine is to me. If we let them, poems also encourage the more difficult notion that your life ought to be as important to me as my own life is; that I can only truly honor and protect myself by honoring and protecting you.

That was my theory. And what I found, on each of the trips making up the national poetry project, which we ended up calling American Conversations, was wildly heartening. We hosted events in public libraries, community centers, rehab facilities, detention centers, churches, retirement homes, and theaters in Alaska, Kentucky, Louisiana, Maine, New Mexico, South Carolina, and South Dakota. We passed out copies of *American Journal*, the anthology I edited for just such a purpose during my time in the laureateship. And then, we'd do the simplest thing: We'd read poems to each other and talk about what we noticed, remembered, wondered, and felt. And we found our way to a counternarrative of careful listening and mutual respect as fostered by poetry. Poems proved to be amazing tools for reminding us of the things we share while also highlighting the differences between us, advocating implicitly for the validity of our differing perspectives.

A nine-year-old girl in New Haven, Kentucky, came by herself to a Saturday morning conversation at her local public library, her home away from home. She sat in the front row with a house key on a string around her neck. She stared up toward the seam between the ceiling and the wall the way children sometimes do when they're thinking. Or she'd look down at her feet or her lap, but not idly;

there was still a kind of attention operating within her body. When she turned to face whoever was speaking, it was as if she wanted to make sure nothing was lost or intercepted on its way to her. Adult women spoke frankly about their memories and their hopes. It was different there now than it had been for them growing up. That this is true of most everyplace doesn't solve the dilemma of how to accept change, and whether or when to push back. How to mourn a loss that comes as an effect of opportunity. What to hope for your kids. When finally she raised her hand, the little girl asked, "When did you realize you had stories to tell?" I told her I was just about her age when I wrote my first poem. Then I asked her, "Do you feel like you have stories to tell?" She nodded and told us one about a teacher in her school. A story—perhaps she realized this then, or has by now, or soon will—about change and loss, pain and need. "You can grow up to be a writer if you want to," I told her. And she nodded, then went back to her listening, which, now that I'm telling it, was exactly how a writer listens.

After an event at Old Summerton High School in South Carolina, one of the public schools desegregated by the US Supreme Court's 1954 *Brown v. Board of Education* decision, Black members of the first integrated graduating class described how they had written poetry back when they were students, and how the poems we'd read and the experience of talking about them with each other had inspired them to reclaim the practice. "I used to fill notebooks," one woman said, and her hands floated up toward her chest as if she was holding one again. How much gets poured onto a page, into a notebook? And how much realer to herself might a person become on the heels of such an act?

A man in the audience at a similar session I was invited to host in

Jackson, Wyoming, raised his hand midway through a conversation to nearly shout, "I get it! When you read a poem, you're just kind of pouring it through your own filter to see what gets caught there. My filter is different from your filter. And different things will get caught in your filter at different times, depending on who and where you are when you read the poem."

Soon after we'd handed out copies of *American Journal* in a juvenile detention center near Juneau, Alaska, a teenager interrupted to ask if we could please read a poem called "Reverse Suicide" by Matt Rasmussen. Just a few moments with the volume in his hands, and it was as if the poem itself had sought him out, offering to provide a fresh vocabulary for talking about the hardest parts of a life.

I will never forget the profound uncertainty I felt at a home for veterans and pioneers about an hour outside of Anchorage, Alaska. Apart from one or two members of the audience, nobody volunteered to speak. I would read a poem, and it would be followed by a longer-than-was-comfortable silence. Sometimes as I was reading, an audience member would audibly groan. It wasn't a reaction I was used to, and it was difficult at times to sit with the long stretches of wordlessness. But afterward, staff members were elated. It turned out that a sizeable portion of the audience was made up of nonverbal residents of the facility's Alzheimer's unit. Those moans and the inaudible movements that accompanied them were concrete indicators of the ways poems had spoken to and gotten through to audience members. Without realizing it, I had been in the presence of a remarkable response to the power of poetry. One thing that has stayed with me from that evening is the realization that the success of such a project didn't hinge upon me performing well or hitting it off with people in these different places; rather, it was about giving people space to engage with poems in their own ways and in the terms most meaningful for them.

There is no formula for reading and responding to poetry. How could there be when the lyric tradition exists in celebration of the individual self and its singular experience of the world? The earliest lyric poems were songs for a single voice. Not the sweeping epics of heroes at war or stranded at sea, but intimate accounts of life's most memorable feelings. Sappho, whose ancient Greek fragments survive from as early as the seventh century BCE, and who would have sung them to the accompaniment of a lyre, bears witness to the particular terms and dimensions of an individual life within the frame of a single moment:

A Girl in Love

"Oh, my sweet mother, 't is in vain,
I cannot weave as once I wove,
So 'wildered is my heart and brain
With thinking of that youth I love."

Perhaps a detail like "I cannot weave as once I wove" offers you just enough of a window into the young speaker's life for you to recognize her hands idle at the loom, and her thoughts adrift in new longing. Whatever it is that draws you in, this momentary brush with a stranger's experience also gifts you with a remembered or an imagined or a wished-for piece of your own. Her heart racing with anticipation carries over for a moment into you.

Almost three thousand years later, it is still a poem's speaker who calls to us from the frame of their singular experience. And what we seek in granting them our attention is decidedly *not* the formulaic, unthinking motions of a prescribed and unchanging rite. No, even when delivering verse in its most methodical traditional forms, like the sestina or the haiku, poetry resists the formulaic in its bid to reawaken us to the miracle and the mystery of our lives. But much of the anxiety surrounding the art form seems to stem from the worry that there exists an authorized way in which a poem ought to be read, and that to set out without such a code of conduct is to be doomed from the outset. One of my hopes in writing this book is to help put such a notion to rest.

How, then, should you go about reading this book and the poems within it? As you might read a letter from a friend, paying eager attention and trusting that much rides on each word. You might also attend to the chapters making up this book as you would a conversation, taking in my thoughts and observations, and also making room to take stock of your own. As someone who has lived most of my life reading, writing, and thinking about poetry, I know there are many points of entry for every poem. Trust the one that speaks to you, and follow where it leads, while also using my perspective as another example of how a poem might be engaged with, contemplated, and discussed.

When it comes to the poems, I suggest you try reading them aloud. How do the sounds of their words and the rhythms of their lines inform your interaction with their images, statements, and the narrative elements they contain? What does the text of a poem call to your attention, and what do you notice, wonder, remember, and feel as a result? There is nothing in a poem that does not wish to be noticed, so starting with this set of general questions will inevitably lead you further into the poem and the world it describes. I usually have to read a poem that is new to me at least twice to feel somewhat oriented within it; afford yourself this opportunity as you move through these chapters. If you can, underline and annotate as you read, so you'll have a lasting roadmap to those areas that caught your initial attention; gradually this document will morph and grow as you revisit these same poems again over time.

My responses to the poems throughout this book are grounded in my response to specific words or phrases, and junctures where the poem's behavior can be seen to shift from one mode or set of terms to another. Grounding your own observations in as much specificity as possible will also give you more to go on; you won't have to speculate about an author's intentions if you can dwell within the concrete particulars of their poem's content. It might also help you to know that, in my own reading practice, if I find myself wandering too far into a tangent—far enough that my own voice seems to become louder or more consequential than the poem itself—I simply quiet myself and return to the poem for grounding. Nearly everything I need for a productive first or second or third encounter with any poem is right there in its lines.

Thematically, the chapters making up this book are built around poetry's capacity to call to a reader's empathy and curiosity, and to mitigate the hindrance of fear. The chapter entitled "Falling Awake: Poetry and the Work of the Unconscious" explores the ways poems equip us to admit and approach life's inevitable uncertainties. It also acknowledges the degree to which poetry, in coaxing a reader to grapple with unresolved questions, helps to activate and affirm faculties of memory, insight, and intuition. The chapter "Any Small Thing Can Save You: On Grief and Accountability" pays close attention to the ways poems help us name and navigate the forms of loss we experience on individual and collective scales. It also highlights poetry's capacity to kindle a productive awareness of the inevitable role that we ourselves play in the losses and upsets endured by others. The chapter "Who Are You?: On Strangers and Others" examines poems that challenge us to look differently at people we've been taught to regard as outside our field of concern; in so doing, poems offer to make us more compassionate toward one another and more recognizable to ourselves. Also running through each chapter are observations about tools in language that allow poems to move, startle, and console us. The book's final chapter, "Be Ye Not Afraid: A Brief Guide to What Poems Are and How They Do What They Do," offers a more detailed discussion of formal craft and elements such as a poem's title, its speaker, its forms of closure, as well as what it means to attempt to assess a work of art like a poem. If you are very new to poetry, or eager for a bit more grounding in elements of the art form, you might want to start there and then go back to the beginning of the book.

Having witnessed how the simple act of reading and talking about poems with others can lead to a sense of trust and ease with one another, I'm left wishing we could make more space for exactly that in our classrooms, in our day-to-day lives, and in the culture we steward together. I wish we could let go some of the need for certainty and the desire to demonstrate our own authority in our interactions with the world. I wish we could abandon the impulse to judge, rate, and rank like incorrigible consumers and instead, together in whatever versions of community we can muster, allow ourselves to wander the wilderness of new feelings—and old feelings in new forms.

I hope you may be inspired to read and reread the poems in the book, and to venture further into the work of the numerous poets cited here. I hope some of you might be inspired to imitate or otherwise respond to the poems discussed here, as a way of leaping into or deepening your own writing practice. Mostly, I hope the voices and imaginations animating the poems in this book, with their questions and their various ways of paying attention, will assure you that your own living, seeking, and witnessing are unique and irreplaceable in the universe.

It is late in our story. We hold tools gleaming and new in trembling hands, and age-old technologies in our whirring minds. What beckons? What waits in the distance ahead?

FALLING AWAKE
Poetry and the Work of the Unconscious

I MUST HAVE BEEN six years old when I was gifted a slim book of poems for children. I remember the red linen bookcloth cover relieved of its dustjacket, and the fine ink drawings alongside each of the poems—in particular the puckered lips and dreamy eyes of the *big baboon by the light of the moon . . . combing his auburn hair.* Spell-like was the effect of this thin compendium, which I pored over that very afternoon as summer light filtered through my bedroom curtains. The beckoning thrum of meter. The affirming chime of rhyme. The delight of recognition and surprise when, all on its own, a poem compelled me to lean close, to learn it, to let it in.

Sometimes a poem can do that—can seem to see you and wave, insisting you have business with each other. On the day I'm remembering, I'm not sure I would have used the word *poem* to describe what I was reading. It was a playful thing to be entertained by. I must have thought that if I could commit it to memory, I'd be able to carry that little bit of enjoyment with me. Perhaps it could even be a way to make someone else happy.

Once the text was good and lodged in my memory, I went looking for my mother. "Listen to this," I said, and stood there brimming. But when I began to recite it, the poem wouldn't let me simply say its words; something about it insisted upon being *delivered*. Take, for instance, the first line, which introduced the characters, and thereby had to be not merely heard, but also seen: "Old Hogan's goat was feeling fine . . ." Could my voice transmit to her the impression of that old, old man working hard in the heat of the day, as I had seen him sketched upon a page in the book? And what about the goat, cunning and willful, unbothered by the burden of responsibility? I jazzed things up—turned "feeling" into *feelin'* and stretched out "fine"—to conjure the free and easy goat as it had filled my mind.

The second line came easily: "Ate six red shirts from off the line." Of their own volition, "six red shirts" sizzled from my tongue, bright as semaphores. If this line were a song, a high-hat cymbal would be activated by each of those words, so you'd feel the scintillation of the goat's crime. And the words "from off the line" would whip in the wind—ta-*dee*, ta-*dee*—as if indifferent to consequence. Deepening my pitch, I continued through to the stanza's closure: "Old Hogan grabbed him by the back / And tied him to the railroad track." It was almost as if the lines themselves enacted a kind of tussle, which was put to rest with the stark finality of rope knotted fast.

Gradually, like a horse working up to a gallop, or a locomotive roaring toward a station, I found myself in the poem's second and final stanza. And I was no longer outside, objective, a messenger and nothing more. I was inside the poem's world, a witness reporting as if from firsthand recollection:

Now when the train came into sight,
That goat grew pale and green with fright.
He heaved a sigh, as if in pain,

at which point, I slowed down. The little bit of empty space, visible trailing the word "pain," commanded silence, suspense. For the flicker of an instant, I allowed my mother to wonder—*Would the train screech to a halt? Would the goat manage to wriggle free? Was this a tale of disaster, or something gentler?*—before serving up the razzmatazz of the final line: "Coughed up those shirts and flagged the train!"

The funny thing about reciting a poem—hearing it as if by way of someone else's listening—is that it becomes, suddenly for you, a different poem. Keying into my mother's reaction, did I sense how the timbre of her own memories might be tinting her view of the text? Did I feel the presence of the stories she sometimes recounted with her own emphasis and flair? Like the one about a country preacher who, wily as a goat, passed from household to household polishing off biscuits and chickens, cakes and whole pies after his all-day Sunday sermons. By which I mean, didn't the tone and tilt of my mother's imagination color the poem for me as I recited it for her? *Mm-hmm*, she might well have said, *if that isn't just like old so-and-so.* . . . Meaning the goat, or the farmer. And I would have been persuaded to agree.

Later, when Mom urged me to repeat the performance for my siblings and our father, nobody thought to ask, *What does it mean?* We were picturing the goat, startled out of his glee by the realization of certain punishment. And the wicked satisfaction of Old Hogan, vindicated finally by the animal's deathly panic. Surely the poem reminded us each of different things. Were we children the goat that our parents, listening, tittered at? Some part of my own imagining was caught up wondering if, like the terrifying Bible story about Abraham and Isaac, Hogan had really wanted to kill his own goat, or if he'd simply wanted to startle him into submission.

Every poem—even one as slight as "Old Hogan's Goat," which charges toward its resolution like a joke toward its punchline—does a portion of its work unconsciously, in the part of the mind from which images and dreams emerge. The part not beholden to explanation, but rather teeming with instinctual knowing, latent memory, deep foreboding. To see the goat. To recognize in it a person you love, or struggle to. To be the train barreling on, unstoppable, toward collision. To borrow the momentary satisfaction of the fed-up farmer, that visceral tug-of-war on the iron tracks. To gloat, and then, perhaps, to make of the poem a lie: To race back to the scene of error, waving a flag, a sheet, the shirt off your own back, in order to save your tormentor, your enemy, your beloved goat. *Forgive me*, you say. *Let us be friends again.* Or to watch it all in the distance as if from a passing train, the strangely familiar pantomime of power, surrender, repentance; the romance of reconciliation.

What purpose does a goat or a train or a fed-up farmer serve in the unconscious mind? The answer is anything, anything they can. Like a mother and the members of a family, and like one's very own child-self, everything you've cared about even briefly, everything you've held and handled in heart or mind, expands the dimensions of your interiority, which abounds not with fixed answers but potential tools—resources of courage and resourcefulness to contend with the freight of fear, longing, isolation, and confusion that is often our human lot. And also joy, love, hope, and gratitude—feelings profound and astonishing enough to require constantly evolving vocabularies. The unconscious mind is, after all, fluent in poetry's leaps and associative shifts, its repetitions, reversals, and counterintuition; they are the very tactics of dream, memory, insight, and premonition.

Above all else, poems enrich the wheelhouse of the unconscious with a wealth of questions. Ask a poem what it means, and it will reply, *Tell me what you noticed.* If, say, you find yourself drawn (as I very much did) to the line, "That goat grew pale and green with fright," the poem might reply, *Perhaps I am useful to fright. See how I helped you to distinguish its features? See what fast thinking the goat's fright fostered?*

Or let's say you find yourself wondering about Old Hogan. Was he hotheaded or simply inflexible? Were those his last six shirts (and why all red)? Was there a Mrs. Hogan? Was the man a widower whose rage was a manifestation of grief? Desperate and alone, what if he was close to tying himself to the tracks? And what if the goat, tender with empathy, is the one who intervened, saving the man? *Already you have surpassed me!* the poem might reply, pleased at the further distance you've managed, all on your own, to travel. *Keep asking questions and we will discover still other things. . . .*

It is curiosity, not foreknowledge, that leads a reader (and a poet, and a poem) beyond the limits of habitual understanding—questions, rather than answers, being the building blocks of insight. Questions, which spring from the unconscious mind's ability to remember, intuit, and speculate (*Was he desperate? Alone? Did he do it out of grief?*), are capable of bridging distances of time, place, allegiance, belief, and any other supposed border used to separate people from one another. Moreover, to form a question is an active creative stance, a way of announcing: *I'm paying attention! I'm ready to observe, remember, intuit!* Curiosity is, at heart, courage; readiness not for a fixed or foretold outcome, but rather a type of uncharted encounter—an adventure.

This de-emphasizing of answers and certainty may seem contrary to some ideas of what poetry is—notions that suppose it to be a form for communicating what the poet already feels and knows, a mode of self-expression rather than self- (and other-) seeking. An off-key question like, *What is the poet trying to say?* has long reinforced the suspicion in many readers' minds that poets have labored to hide and distort otherwise familiar information within their poems. As a result, concrete images, as well as metaphors and similes a reader can readily access via sensory impressions, are construed into *symbols* by the reader trained to hunt for puzzles, secrets, and obfuscation in the lines of poems. Although this trend is thankfully waning, generations of students encountering poems on exams have been goaded into approaching poems with the desire to unlock something like a secret code, believing that if they succeed, the poem's definitive interpretation will light up or come tumbling out in reward. This approach has caused many readers to engage in counterproductive cognitive struggle with the many sensory details loaded into the lines of poems—details yearning not to be decoded but rather *felt*. And in reality, much of the pleasure of poetry across periods and traditions lies not in answers but an explicit or subtly resonant *unknowing*. What do I mean? While every poem guides a reader to notice certain concrete elements, it also engages with forms of abstraction and ambiguity—details that charge the poem's "facts" with additional psychic weight and emotional tone. Oftentimes it is a productive engagement with the nature of uncertainty and irresolution that accounts for a poem's staying power.

Take "Those Winter Sundays," by Robert Hayden, which describes a childhood memory with visceral clarity:

Those Winter Sundays

> Sundays too my father got up early
> and put his clothes on in the blueblack cold,
> then with cracked hands that ached
> from labor in the weekday weather made
> banked fires blaze. No one ever thanked him.
>
> I'd wake and hear the cold splintering, breaking.
> When the rooms were warm, he'd call,
> and slowly I would rise and dress,
> fearing the chronic angers of that house,
>
> Speaking indifferently to him,
> who had driven out the cold
> and polished my good shoes as well.
> What did I know, what did I know
> of love's austere and lonely offices?

From its opening line, the poem quietly suggests that the nature of memory is not linear and discrete, but rather ongoing: a matter of unfinished business. One of the first gestures that alerts me to this sense of ongoingness is the word "too" in the poem's first line: "Sundays too my father got up early" welcomes a reader into what is not the beginning of a story, but rather a cycle or a loop of recurrence.

And there are other surprising ways of marking time in the poem.

The sense of the word "early" is further fleshed out with the image of "blueblack cold." In the absence of definite markers like hours and season, a reader is made to feel or sense their way into an awareness of the poem's setting. We are not so much in a specific time as in a circumstance: of dark, of chill, of "cracked hands that ached / from labor in the weekday weather." Vowel and consonant sounds in the stanza—"blueblack," "cracked," "ached," and "blaze"—further underscore the emotional terms of the speaker's circumstance: it is brittle, brutal, combustible.

The musical behavior of language in the first stanza makes way for the sensory dimension of hearing to enter into the second. When the speaker says, "I'd wake and hear the cold splintering, breaking," I am reminded of the different ways that memory can be activated and deepened. Sight is one sense that activates memory, but so are hearing and smell. How often are you drawn back into another age or stage of your own life by a song or a whiff of fragrance? These senses are like keys to the various chambers of the unconscious. The sound of a room warming, and the rousing effect of rising temperature upon the waking body, draw the reader more fully into the scene; they also facilitate the speaker's further descent into recollection, until finally the stanza arrives at a direct declaration of emotional climate: "fearing the chronic angers of that house." And like "too" in the poem's opening line, "chronic" is a temporal word; it serves to reaffirm the cyclical nature of time and experience. What the poem is pondering is a pattern in which the speaker was once—and perhaps, owing to memory, still is—held.

There is so little about which the poem's reader is allowed to feel indifferent in this poem, and that has everything to do with the emotional tone abounding in its images and verbs. But the fullest portrait of the speaker arrives in the poem's final stanza, beginning with the line: "Speaking indifferently to him." *Indifferently?* It's hard to imagine that the speaker would have been indifferent to "the chronic angers of that house"; after all, he feared them. Perhaps, then, indifference is an affect, a coping mechanism. Also telling is the way this sentence continues across subsequent lines, admitting a fuller acknowledgment of the father's obedience to his duties as a parent:

> to him,
> who had driven out the cold
> and polished my good shoes as well.

Is the poem's speaker in the process of calculating something like a debt owed? If this is the case, then his father's efforts to drive out the cold and polish his son's good shoes can be added to a column with similar acts of generosity, like rising early and making "banked fires blaze." On the other side of the balance is the father's portion of "the chronic angers of that house." But how much did—or does—the speaker owe? Is this acknowledgment of indebtedness part of what the poem has set out to confront?

As I read, I find that I become more than a witness to what is being recollected; I also begin to accept a portion of the speaker's self-scrutinizing. Fresh pangs of regret from my own youth flash in my mind. The time I made my mother wait in the car while I toured a college campus, because I feared being seen as a child in the care of a parent. And because I wanted to be free. *Free!* And how selfish I felt, returning after those exhilarating hours, to find her quietly reading a book in the driver's seat. The countless times I scowled and asked my father to turn off his music as we rode long distances together in the family Ford. My many childish silences and the resentments from which they sprang as I neared the age of leaving home for the first and again for the second time. As if in empathy with the poem's speaker, I become aware of a retrospective shame at the selfishness of these and other instances of my own past behavior, even as I am aware that my parents—having once been young themselves—must have seen the fuller picture. I wonder: Did the debts I accrued while in their care recall for them the debts and apologies their own young selves owed their parents? These are not new memories, but my new questions about them, and my willingness to confront and own them rather than to merely cringe them back into the further recesses of my mind, have arrived by way of my current encounter with Hayden's poem.

But it is the poem's closure, which articulates an insistent yet unanswered question, that pulls the poem from the contained space of remembering and into the larger emotional work of reckoning. The apex of feeling dwells in the insistence and vulnerability of the poem's penultimate line: "What did I know, what did I know." The broadening out into an unanswered question, rather than narrowing to the point of a fixed answer, is a prime source of the poem's emotional amplitude. That depth of emotion, augmented by something like the heartbeat of repetition, is contrasted by the composure and quite nearly clinical tone of the final line: "of love's austere and lonely offices?" It is as if we've been led to a place from which an overwhelming emotional susceptibility can be glimpsed—yet we're held back from plunging in. Something about that dynamic mimics the irresolution, in life, of not always being able to go back and make things right. And how has the poem's speaker come to understand that love's "offices" are "austere and lonely" if not from his own growth and struggle, his own service to devotions for which he has or has not been adequately thanked? Might unresolved complexities in his own present life be one reason why the past is on the speaker's mind? Certainly the poem's form—a sonnet—insists upon a turn or reversal in thought or argument. In this case, the pivot away from fear, resentment, and emotional withholding and toward empathy feels like an emotional revolution. In Hayden's hands, the sonnet form, traditionally a vehicle for expressions of romantic love, becomes a means of revisiting and reenvisioning the convolutions of familial love.

Each word of the poem's closing line is familiar, but operating together, they assemble the terms of a new, or newly perceived, emotional condition—one charged with the contradictions of intimacy and formality, isolation and need, drudgery and care. Think how different the poem would have become had the final question ended not upon the conundrum of "love's austere and lonely offices," but rather the pat certitude of a more logically familiar phrase like "how thankless the job of parenting can be." I think my readerly heart and mind would have slammed shut, disappointed that such careful observation and courageous self-searching had led to nothing more than an empty platitude or pat truism. The poem remains challenging and compelling precisely because of its willingness to be anchored not in emotional composure, but rather in the speaker's deep pang of unexpressed gratitude. In this sense, the poem authorizes me to consider my own pangs—and, in the very same moment, to admit my role in the pangs of others. What a productive form of introspection! Hayden's speaker grants me access to chambers of my own unconscious against which my waking mind has long labored to protect itself. Am I punished? Am I traumatized? I think, rather, that I'm enlarged by the speaker's wish to recognize and admit more than ought to be possible for a lone self operating within the limits of an ordinary life. I am persuaded to remember—*yes, I know this; how do I know this?*—that there are points in every life where a person becomes more than their usual self. Split seconds where the improbable becomes actual. Feats of uncharacteristic strength, or strength of character. We surprise ourselves. We defy pat summary. Poetry is an art form through which we might better recognize and appreciate the circumstances under which you and I remain—even to ourselves—a kind of mystery.

A POEM'S CAPACITY TO dwell or hover for brief or long periods in ambiguity or irresolution is what nineteenth-century British Romantic poet John Keats termed Negative Capability: "when man is capable of being in uncertainties, mysteries, doubts, without any irritable reaching after fact and reason." I don't read Keats as arguing that a reader ought simply to accept that bumping up against mystery or uncertainty should signal the end of the line, a sign to throw up one's hands and seek no further. Rather, I take him to mean that occasional barriers to certainty and resolution in a poem and in a life are an invitation to exercise different faculties of discernment and perception.

We can find evidence of such a shift in strategy in Keats's "To Autumn," an ode* written in address to the season of harvests and plenitude. Gradually the poem begins to shift from an emphasis on the "more, / And still more" of autumn's bounty to anticipate the moment when the season of plenty will end. But instead of turning

---

* An ode is a lyric poem written in praise of and in address to someone or something.

to a contemplation of winter, the final of the poem's three stanzas inquires after "the songs of spring":

> Where are the songs of spring? Ay, Where are they?
>   Think not of them, thou hast thy music too,—
> While barred clouds bloom the soft-dying day,
>   And touch the stubble-plains with rosy hue;
> Then in a wailful choir the small gnats mourn
>   Among the river sallows, borne aloft
>   Or sinking as the light wind lives or dies;
> And full-grown lambs loud bleat from hilly bourn;
>   Hedge-crickets sing; and now with treble soft
>   The red-breast whistles from a garden-croft;
>   And gathering swallows twitter in the skies.

Let's start with the stanza's opening question: "Where are the songs of spring? Ay, Where are they?" Is it really a question, at all? It's not a matter of seeking information so much as announcing an absence, a longing. It's a sigh. A way of acknowledging the intractability of goodbye. And what might it mean to wonder after a song, which doesn't *go* anywhere so much as end? How much else in life just—*poof*—disappears? The figure "Where are the songs of spring? Ay, Where are they?" captures the psychological shock arising from the fact that something can be emphatically present one moment and utterly vanished the next; it tips the poem into questions of loss and finality, and empowers the speaker to take recourse to faculties not of knowledge, for fact is of little consolation in the face of loss, but of feeling and unconscious knowing.

In life, when mystery, doubt, and quiet fear rear up, our habit is to seek the assurance of answers, strategies, expert advice. We hedge our bets, make contingency plans, cleave to platitudes. We do what it takes to stay materially and emotionally afloat. But poetry is a different kind of enterprise, one engaged with the deep reserves of wisdom, memory, and emotional wherewithal every one of us possesses. And so rather than neatening up a state of quandary or denying inevitability, a poem might seek to operate from within these very circumstances.

I'd even argue that the presence of rhyme helps push the poem toward images and statements that veer away from predictable expectation. Because a person doesn't naturally think in rhyme, the expression of an idea can't simply follow an instinctual or habitual path; it must, instead, flow through the vowels and consonants compatible with the poem's established sonic patterns. Keats reasons differently in rhyming verse than he would, say, in the prose of a letter. His decision to write "the small gnats mourn" in line five of the stanza pushes him, in turn, to scour the (real, remembered, or imagined) scene for images and words that sustain the music of the poem. The music of rhyme is one explanation for why the reader's attention is drawn toward the lambs up near the "hilly bourn," or hillside stream. By this same constraint, the stanza becomes filled with "songs" and forms of "music" that are not rooted in sound, like the "rosy hue" of clouds at sunset, and the visual patterns of birds in flight, "borne aloft" or dipping upon the wind.

Keats's speaker redirects attention back toward the season at hand, asking what autumn's still-present music is made of. But with the larger question of mortality still hanging in the air, so much of what he sees—the many ambient descriptions populating the stanza—resonate with forebodings of death. I'm thinking of gestures like "the soft-dying day" and the "wailful choir" in which "the small gnats mourn," all of which augur seasonal change, yes, but also something more like human bereavement. Even the noun "sallows," which in the poem's context is another name for willow trees, also manages to conjure in the reader's mind the pallor of sickly skin. Of course, these ordinary features of the landscape don't always augur death; they take on this tinge because death is on the speaker's mind.

If, instead of writing a poem, Keats had been discussing the topic of mortality with a friend, he may have been talked back from the rails: *Don't think that way! Focus on the joy and pleasure life has to offer!* Even if he'd had good reason to worry about dying (and Keats did; by the time he wrote "To Autumn," he'd lost both his mother and brother to tuberculosis, the condition to which he, too, would eventually succumb), any good friend might have assured him, *You have a long, happy life ahead of you.* It's what friends do. But a poem is a different kind of confidant, one willing to accompany you even into unspeakable regions of awareness. *Are you afraid of death?* a poem will ask. *Let's talk about it. Let's touch it with our minds.*

As the stanza continues in observation of the landscape, it's through a perspective given over fully to mourning. Yes, I see hills cresting and dipping. Yes, I can make out lambs, crickets, and robins in their habitats. But foregrounded in my perception are terms like "borne aloft," "sinking," and "lives or dies," which have become by now utterly funereal in connotation. So much so that the ordinary music of the season—the bleating lambs, the singing crickets and robins—all have become a chorus of mourners in my ear. And while there is also music in the poem's final image of "swallows [that] twitter in the skies," what that line serves chiefly to conjure for me is the presence of something "gathering" in the distance to approach. The small birds become a force approaching with a somber finality, like pallbearers, to bear away (or "aloft") the deceased. Most startling for me in this final line is the "twitter" the birds' presence makes. Putting aside the social media platform formerly called Twitter (which, granted, may have its own ominous connotations for a twenty-first-century reader), the verb suggests such a delicate, ordinary sound. Is this—could it be?—how lightly our human losses are taken by the natural world? Is this—could it be?—how death itself operates? Not as a massive wave or a great gale, but as a presence that approaches softly to carry us off?

For me, an initial reading of a poem like this one lands easily in the terms of an individual imagination, a single life. Mine, perhaps, or one that may be relevant or useful to mine. But when I approach the poem a second time, I can decipher its relevance to a collective apprehension. After all, the landscape itself is viewed not in individual terms, but by way of collectives. The gnats, the river sallows, the lambs, the crickets, and of course the swallows—all are taken not singly but as species upon the earth. What if I allow the poem to activate an awareness of their mortality as well? What if, say, the mournful gnats are not metaphorical manifestations of human grief, but agents possessed of their very own feelings? What if these "full-grown lambs loud bleat[ing]" are crying for their own gone mothers, and for themselves, too, bred to be sold and slaughtered? The pastoral scene becomes the opposite of a container for a predictable human fear: It is permitted to act as a warning or an apology for the gathering shadow of human devastation upon a living landscape. Processing "To Autumn" in this way is to approach a vocabulary of collective conscience. It is a way of looking past what I may want to see and toward what I need to know. By this reading, I am guided to recognize the extent to which it is not fate at all but rather human enterprise that hunts and herds and hauls away the songs of spring.

TO ENGAGE WITH A poem is an active—even a creative—pursuit. The narrative or dramatic situation swells around you, gathering you up in the poem's emotional weather. You see and feel the effects of images. You pay close attention to the ways verbs serve to animate and characterize the scene. You surrender to the language-made music binding these and other things into the unity of the poem. And even as you do all of this to participate fully in the world of the poem, you're also using the poem as a means of moving toward other ranges of experience: what you remember, what you fear, what you recognize from elsewhere. Managing all of this at once, you might find yourself pausing for a moment to follow a tangent to its conclusion before turning your attention back to the forward unfolding of the poem itself. All of this is productive! All of this affirms that the experience of reading is, ideally, an act of co-activation, even of co-creation—a matter of feeling, thinking, and harmonizing across space and time with another human whose proxy is the poem itself.

What I am describing isn't simply a literary operation; it's a set of essential life skills—faculties of attention and imagination that fortify us to withstand the ripples and torrents of our own individual and collective narratives. When a poem draws observation of the external world into direct dialogue with its speaker's internal delight or unrest, it is inviting us to exercise skills critical to the integration of such things as mind and body, the rational and feeling selves, and the individual ego's accountability to others. This is why I am always perplexed by the indefatigable question, *Does poetry matter?* Why not ask, Does memory matter? Does resilience matter? Do anxiety, hope, courage, wisdom, and emotional stamina matter? Does disaster matter, and our ability to withstand it? Does joy? How much of a matter is grief in the course of a life, a nation, a world? Engaging with a poem is one way of strengthening our ability to do something with these powerful feelings. Not to freeze or recoil. Not to shun or deny. But to admit, withstand, rethink—even to act. It's possible that the motivation behind a question like *Does poetry matter?* arises out of the conception that poetry is a narrow niche, a selfish respite from the practical demands of day-to-day life. But to care about poetry is to listen in earnest to another's testimony, and to draw that awareness in toward your own emotional fortitude, imagination, patience, and empathy. To care about poetry is to attend to a host of complex faculties that equip you to consider yourself alongside and in light of equally worthy others.

That constant interplay between self-regard and a consideration of others has, for most of human history, been common practice. Kin, tribe, community, state. To exist within such constructs has long meant trusting others to watch over or provide, while also accepting that such a guarantee comes with a reciprocal duty to the group. But this model has been increasingly tempered by more a recent fixation upon the self and its primacy, evident perhaps nowhere more emphatically than in the twenty-first-century marketplace for products and services promising individual comfort and protection, personal authority, and whole spectrums of indulgence and self-aggrandizement. So convincing is the sales pitch that to shirk a duty to *Me*, *My*, *Self*, and *I* has come to bear the taint of dereliction. Think of the many tools that have emerged to minimize the bother of strangers: Selfie sticks. Self-checkout lanes. Noise-canceling headphones. Smart phones buzzing and singing with updates gloriously curated to individual appetites and needs. Strangers have been so thoroughly framed as a hassle and a distraction that online decorum permits us to rank, critique, correct, berate, and even eventually block them. Through it all, the island of self, though lashed by inevitable waves of intrusion, stands solid and secure.

Or does it? Our current moment is also marked by new heights of anxiety and depression, social division, misinformation, and mistrust. Add to that a fear of the stranger and a demonization of the "other," which tendencies often enough bring lethal repercussions. There are so many incentives in our culture to engage in outrage, stand our ground, withhold empathy, and snuff out dialogue. Clickbait aimed at amping up fear and self-righteousness. Phrases coded to authorize the wholesale denigration of entire groups of people. Upticks in extremist rhetoric and violence. The phobia that our nation must be reclaimed, lest it go somewhere, lest some nefarious group succeed in taking it away. But poetry—which draws our feelings and attention out toward myriad other lives, and also in for a fuller accounting of our own innate capacities—is one means of tempering and even disrupting our susceptibility to a slew of atomizing, alienating tendencies.

A poem—one you might read, or one you may endeavor to write—forges a pathway in toward an autonomous and inexhaustible region of yourself endowed with patience, courage, and discernment surpassing what may rise to the surface in the course of an ordinary day. A poem—one you might recall only in fragments—invites such close attention to subtle particularities as to disarm the blunt, bullish part of yourself disposed to hot takes and livid tirades. A poem—any poem that slows you down, draws you in and invites you to recognize, wonder, and remember—is a gateway to the inner life: the unique, uncompromised, unincorporated, unmappable territory we each possess and by which (as with a wormhole) we are connected to all that is. Do you—can you—believe you are possessed of such a space? If not, why? As the world we share becomes increasingly demarcated into territories and domains; as it is further zoned and branded into exclusive spaces welcoming to some, hostile to others, and off-limits at some inevitable juncture to you or to me; as the dominion of the increasingly few over the much and the many further unfolds, how important is it—how critical—to understand there is and has always been, for each of us, a wilderness within?

Does poetry matter? Why not ask does imagination matter? How about patience, courage, humility, hope, and awe? Do we value these traits? Do we prize a world in which they exist? Poetry matters in so many ways that I've begun to suspect the question itself—*Does poetry matter?*—must be a ploy intended to swindle us out of the fundamental human capacities from which the art form emerges and to which it continues to bear witness.

SOMETIMES, A POEM CHARGES my way as if from across an epic expanse, shattering my comfortable view of the world and my usual place within it. A poem like a raucous herd thundering the ground as the distance between it and me diminishes. To feel the borders of my own self ruptured. To be held in the center of a furor as all but awe and recognition fall away. The first time I encountered the work of poet Joy Harjo, a feeling more powerful than appreciation befell me—I'd call it, rather, transmutation. As her poems constituted themselves around me, it was as if I became both stampede and terrain. I even became the small pebbles leaping up from the earth as if to say, *Take me with you!* Her poems went beyond calling me to attention; they challenged me to claim and to use feelings of vulnerability and states of conflict both in experiencing the text and in looking up, after the poem was over, at the world and myself.

"She Had Some Horses" is a five-part poem sequence in Harjo's 1983 book of the same title. I'd like to engage with the first and most widely anthologized section of the sequence whose momentum and iconoclastic authority leap easily beyond the forms of reasoning and decorum sometimes prized in poems, and toward a poetics of paradox, simultaneity, insistence, and revelation. I turn to it now as an example of how a poem can allow its reader to be in several places at once, transcending logic and linearity. Among the many other things "She Had Some Horses" accomplishes is to draw its reader into what is both individual and collective history, blurring or implicitly arguing against any distinction between the two. Moreover, the poem insists upon the reader's collaboration. Like all great poetry, it is not a mere object for consumption, but a creative proposition requesting our full participation. We feel, remember, and reflect across space and time alongside another imagination by way of the poem:

She Had Some Horses

She had some horses.

She had horses who were bodies of sand.
She had horses who were maps drawn of blood.
She had horses who were skins of ocean water.
She had horses who were the blue air of sky.
She had horses who were fur and teeth.
She had horses who were clay and would break.
She had horses who were splintered red cliff.

She had some horses.

She had horses with eyes of trains.
She had horses with full, brown thighs.
She had horses who laughed too much.
She had horses who threw rocks at glass houses.
She had horses who licked razor blades.

She had some horses.

She had horses who danced in their mothers' arms.
She had horses who thought they were the sun and their bodies shone and burned like stars.
She had horses who waltzed nightly on the moon.
She had horses who were much too shy, and kept quiet in stalls of their own making.

She had some horses.

She had horses who liked Creek Stomp Dance songs.
She had horses who cried in their beer.
She had horses who spit at male queens who made them afraid of themselves.
She had horses who said they weren't afraid.
She had horses who lied.
She had horses who told the truth, who were stripped bare of their tongues.

She had some horses.

She had horses who called themselves, "horse."
She had horses who called themselves, "spirit," and kept
their voices secret and to themselves.
She had horses who had no names.
She had horses who had books of names.

She had some horses.

She had horses who whispered in the dark, who were
 afraid to speak.
She had horses who screamed out of fear of the silence, who
carried knives to protect themselves from ghosts.
She had horses who waited for destruction.
She had horses who waited for resurrection.

She had some horses.

She had horses who got down on their knees for any savior.
She had horses who thought their high price had saved
 them.
She had horses who tried to save her, who climbed in her
bed at night and prayed.

She had some horses.

She had some horses she loved.
She had some horses she hated.

These were the same horses.

Often it is the way we talk about poetry that teaches us what to expect from the art form, and so I want to celebrate the ways this poem manages to defy conventional logic in so much of its behavior. Rather than narrating a linear sequence or complying with a reader's wish to know such things as who is speaking and from what immediate circumstance, the poem occludes its speaker, conflates all of its many distinct characters into the figure of "horses," and concerns itself chiefly with its own questions. In other words, it knows better than to give me what I arrive thinking I might want. And yet I come away as from a profoundly generous, vulnerable exchange with someone I've only just met, but whom I already know and trust. It strikes me as essential to acknowledge the willful nature inherent in the art form, and to celebrate the ingenious disobedience of which every poem is capable. Isn't it, after all, precisely the desire to be led past expected bounds of habit and convention—habit and convention being insufficient harbors for our most urgent and confounding feelings—that leads us to the threshold of a poem?

Eight one-line stanzas, made up of the sentence "She had some horses," recur at intervals as if to measure and punctuate a reader's movement through the poem. Each new set of images and recollections follows upon this repeated refrain, which assures (and insists) that we readers know where we are because we've been there before. But Harjo challenges us, as well. Each time I reencounter the touchstone "She had some horses," it is on the heels of a stanza cataloging distinct states of desire and abandon, tenderness and fear, insistence and surrender that have been witnessed, inflicted, and endured. In such a context, the refrain operates much like a liturgical response, guiding us back to the contained terms of a known rite before and after each new plunge into fresh revelation.

Alternating with the poem's one-line stanzas are two- to eight-line anaphora (or list-based) stanzas, which bring on a kind of acceleration. For one thing, their visual repetition makes them appear to stream down the page, the way the numbers on a slot machine blur into pure spin. They also take us places and spill out fragments of several recollected relationships and encounters. To arrive in each one after the terse composure of a refrain-based stanza is to be gripped anew by a quickening of body and mind.

The poem's second stanza, with its opening line, "She had horses who were bodies of sand," sideswipes the expectation of encountering animals, and offers instead the vista of a landscape: "sand," "cliff," "air," "water," and "sky." But just as Keats's descriptions of the autumn landscape introduce the anxiety of death into his poem "To Autumn," Harjo's descriptions of the environment activate terms useful to the forms of conflict of which her poem is mindful. There are "maps drawn of blood," "splintered red cliff[s]," and "clay" we are told "would break." This landscape is permeated with evidence of contestation. In such close proximity to "blood," "break," and "splintered," even the stanza's seemingly neutral images—"blue air of sky" and "fur and teeth"—absorb intimations of past or future struggle. "Blue" alongside "air" startles me into an awareness of breathlessness and the threat of asphyxiation, while "fur and teeth" hints at the sense of bodily—of animal—combat. Though little narrative evidence invites me to go much further with these impressions, the stanza doesn't seek to operate narratively. The images are like flashes of lightning—or like memories and premonitions—augmenting the stanza's already palpable foreboding.

Stanza four stirs with the activity of bodies, inviting the energy and commotion of life to charge into the poem. The image "She had horses with eyes of trains"* insists upon being pondered. Do the "eyes of trains" glow cold or bright? Do they race past, or mimic the gaze of someone studying the distance? The poem dissuades me from trying to nail down these details; instead, its rapid-fire listing urges me to take in everything and—like the images themselves—keep moving forward. When I do, I'm rewarded with the internal rhyme of "eyes" with "thighs" in the next line, and the sensuality not only of bodies but of lives in action—the abandon of "laugh[ing] too much," the recklessness of throwing "rocks at glass houses," and the dangerous thrill of "lick[ing] razor blades." The stanza locates me in the presence of characters living willfully and impulsively, no matter the consequences.

In subsequent stanzas, recklessness is replaced with something like tactical ingenuity. The ability to name and define oneself is seized rather than given freely, improvised rather than guaranteed. The parameters by which characters find or allow themselves to be constrained can be seen to expand and contract from "their mother's arms," to the literal cosmos, to "stalls of their own making." I am not sure, for example, who is more autonomous: the "horses who had no names" or the ones "who had books of names"; those "who called themselves 'horse,'" or those "who called themselves 'spirit' and kept / their voices secret and to themselves." Perhaps this is the point. In order to avoid being squeezed into smaller and smaller possibilities, some must hide or disguise themselves and the freedoms they seek. For Harjo, a Muscogee (Creek) poet invested in Native Nations traditions, the presence of these tensions in the poem may be inviting

---

* When the poem was originally published, this line appeared as "She had horses with long, pointed breasts."

readers to make more, not less, of the terms of history mingled in the poem. Histories in which war has been waged and treaties bungled in the struggle to overwrite age-old maps. Histories of forced relocation and hard-won endurance in which citizens of Tribal nations were routinely "stripped / bare" of their land, homes, children, languages, and more by an occupying presence.

Maybe now is a good time to look more closely at the poem's many "horses." Ought they to be taken as literal, or something else? When I'm asked to nail down an ambiguity in any poem, I often first ask my students or readers what possibilities they themselves discern from the presence of dichotomy or multiplicity in a poem. Oftentimes, poems are instigated by the ways commonplace feelings defy our expectations—how sometimes love and conflict, say, can even overlap or bleed into one another. In situations like these, the poem, like a first responder, might go straight to the heart of disorientation, bringing fresh attention to areas of perplexity, inviting the reader to ponder the relationship between seemingly disparate or incompatible states—or even the feeling of being stranded on the emotional border between one and another. I'm of the opinion that a poem's ambiguities are not so much looking to win out over one another as simply to be felt and considered. What does the possibility of literal horses bring to your reading of the poem? What do real horses there in the poem's lines cause you to sense, feel, anticipate, remember, and wonder? What floods into your own body at these junctures in the poem as visceral sensation or muscle memory?

Some of what the horses impart for me is exhilaration, mystery, grace, and strength. They are both mythic and familiar; even a wild horse invites, in most people, the fleeting hope of connection and understanding. I know how small I've felt standing near a horse, looking up into the intelligence of its eyes, aware of the wild power its muscled body harbors. In Harjo's poem, horses are always plural; never does the poem make mention of a lone horse. And so I think of families, of nations, of a whole landscape marked by and belonging to herds and herds of horses. I think of the way a horse can be utterly still and appear to study you as if deciding something. And how the next instant, it can seem to summon a whole new kind of weather as it sprints away. Have I ever thought of horses betraying or disappointing one another? Not until this poem offered me examples of these and other relational dynamics, which augment my sense of the independence and complexity—and even the particular desperations—of an animal I have been habituated to understanding solely in terms of its instinct and training.

And if I take the poem's horses as people? To be honest, it is always my habit to look for corollaries to the human world in poems. When I seek the presence of people in Harjo's lines, the human figures that emerge appear abstract, archetypal, legible most vividly as dynamics of power and submission, will and need. But the repetition of the phrase "She had" reminds me again and again that any horses that were once situated in the *here and now* of the poem are gone. In their place are memories, like abandoned landscapes. The image of horses makes that absence feel grand and cinematic: setting sun, swirling dust, all traces of presence gone save for hoofprints, the earth worn into grooves and gullies. As if joy and ache have disappeared in the way a herd of horses might: via stampede.

In her introduction to the 2008 reissue of *She Had Some Horses*, Harjo remarks that the question she most hears from readers of her work is, "What do the horses mean?" And while she doesn't see it as "the poet's work to reduce the poem from poetry to logical sense," she does state:

> Like most poets, I don't really know what my poems or the stuff of my poetry means *exactly*. That's not the point. It never was the point. I am aware of stepping into a force field or dream field of language, of sound. Each journey is different, just as the ocean or the sky is never the same from one day to another. I am engaged by the music, by the deep. And I go until the poem and I find each other. Sometimes I go by horseback.

Like so much of what the poem enacts, Harjo describes her process of writing as a relational pursuit, one in which the poet and the entity that is the poem are seeking one another. When I consider the possibilities of "a force field or dream field of language," I think of energy, the unconscious mind, and the ways language accrues different forms of power and resonance when it veers away from a strictly logical behavior. Metaphor. Sound-sense: the moods, emotional tenors, and connotations that emerge by way of the sonic qualities of language. Not knowledge, but a *knowing* that extends from regions of memory and insight transcending lived or earned experience.

Harjo also acknowledges that she descends from a culture of people who "came to know horses":

> I understand there was some exchange of power between the horse people and my relatives from seven generations or more back. I am the seventh generation from Monahwee (sometimes spelled as "Menawa"), who is still a beloved person to the Mvskoke people, my tribal nation. I was told how he had a

way with horses. He could speak with them. He also knew how to bend time. He could leave for a destination by horseback at the same time as his cohorts, then arrive at his destination long before it was physically possible to arrive.

Perhaps horses—and horseback—in Harjo's poetic imagination are gateways to regions of consciousness and memory that aren't walled in or limned by the span of a single lifetime. Perhaps Harjo's horses—and poetry itself—might be a conduit between the finite self and the immeasurable whole. There is even the feeling of welcome rupture that enters via her recollection of encounters with actual horses:

> And there was the horse that came to see me once in the middle of a long drive north from Las Cruces, New Mexico, to Albuquerque. I perceived him first by an ancient and familiar smell. Then I was broken open by memory when he nudged me, in that space that is always around and through us, a space not defined or bound by linear time or perception.

The sudden deep recognition. The feeling of breaking open and being tipped into a space "around and through" that is impervious to the human view of linear time and the appearance of things as separate from one another. In this instance of Harjo's prose, I recognize as concise and felicitous a statement about the art of poetry as any. I'm also reminded of something Albert Einstein described numerous times and in varying ways as mankind's "optical delusion":

> A human being is a part of the whole, called by us "Universe," a part limited in time and space. He experiences himself, his

thoughts and feelings as something separated from the rest—a kind of optical delusion of his consciousness. This delusion is a kind of prison for us, restricting us to our personal desires and to affection for a few persons nearest to us. Our task must be to free ourselves from this prison by widening our circle of compassion to embrace all living creatures and the whole nature in its beauty. Nobody is able to achieve this completely, but the striving for such achievement is in itself a part of the liberation and a foundation for inner security.

To engage with poetry in a vigorous and wholehearted fashion strikes me as one way to sense one's position in the universe as a point of convergence with all else. I don't doubt Einstein when he calls the complete mastery of such a state an impossibility. Even so, a poem like "She Had Some Horses" brings readers close to a momentary taste of universal continuity, in part by tampering with the fixity of that bedrock of mankind's "delusion": linear time.

Though set in the past tense, the poem teems with dynamic presence, as if all of its glimpses into the once-ago somehow remain active even now. And so there is the thrill and the threat of sensing we, in solidarity with the poem's "She," could be hauled back to harms and upsets it has pained us to endure, attachments we've labored to sever, even losses we've only lately finished grieving. Similarly, the poem collapses the distance between public and private, intimate and collective. The merging of these scales is seamless in a line like "She had horses who whispered in the dark, who were afraid to speak," which transmits the understanding that no space is wholly intimate, and that dissent—between lovers, between family members, between citizens and the state—is always punishable.

Considered alongside the Einstein proposition, Harjo's poem causes me to admit how complicated—even how potentially threatening—some forms of compassion must seem. Perhaps the "prison" Einstein describes is one many of us, out of fear, have chosen.

Why fear? One answer that comes to mind is that fear has been taught to us. We compete not to share but to win the spoils of wealth, power, and regard. To win—to succeed—in the terms enforced by the global marketplace is to carve out a larger solitude, to build out the moat surrounding ourselves from the encroachment of others and the threats or demands we imagine they'll come bearing. Does it feel better to inhabit even an imperfect oasis knowing that someone looks on in envy of what we possess? Our time, our belongings, the lifestyles we claim to lead? To be up near the top of the many hierarchies to which we submit. To lean out from that position to glimpse others occupying altitudes less desirable than our own. To believe it possible and desirable to ascend to a solitude even beyond vulnerability itself (though isn't it when we find ourselves most alone that vulnerability reminds us of its staying power?). What would it cost us to exit such a scheme and enter into a dynamic of genuine compassion—suffering together as equals with every living other, sharing their joy, and seeking to tend to their unrest—across the infinite sweep of the universe? That's a big question to try and answer, even to thoroughly ponder. But what if we could test versions of such compassion at the scale of a single poem?

Before closing, the poem's focus constricts around the dual presence of piety and threat:

> She had horses who tried to save her, who climbed in her
> bed at night and prayed.

The struggle to buck the smothering patterns of histories both public and private is a large part of what constitutes vulnerability throughout this poem, and so I'm struck by the dissonance between these two phrases: "tried to save her" and "climbed in her / bed at night." What would it mean for horses—friends or enemies or perhaps even entities with the power of a nation at their command—to climb into her bed at night? For what purpose? To what or whom would they pray? I'd go so far as to say that the homonym *preyed* becomes quietly audible as such a scene takes shape, bringing with it something like the ghost of the originally published version of these lines: ". . . who climbed in her / bed at night and prayed as they raped her." Even so, the poem resists outrage. Is this, I wonder, why the reference to rape has been revised away? Because being tipped into outrage could permit some to settle into the notion that the people who have hurt us cease to belong to the human, let alone the Universal, family? Cooly, almost like a song, or a dream, the poem invites us, its readers, past fear, past the tit for tat of conventional wisdom, and toward the challenge of radical union:

> She had some horses she loved.
> She had some horses she hated.
>
> These were the same horses.

Harjo's poem calls to mind the numerous forms of estrangement we choose, or even merely tolerate, over the span of a lifetime. How we can sometimes find ourselves drifting away from people, places, and habits that once seemed essential in order to disencumber ourselves from what is no longer beneficial. How other such ruptures—changes we fight against or for—are more painful or hard-won. And how it is occasionally possible to come away from both forms of change with a capacity for acceptance similar to that which animates the poem's world-rearranging final line.

And what about the quieter estrangements—the ones that function to lead us away from our innermost selves, away from the terms by which our own most deeply rooted feelings and intentions can be discerned and heeded? The gentle slide by which our psychic or emotional grounding can go from being solid to murky. A subtle muffling of the intuition. A fissure widening between us and ourselves. Most of the time, we may not even be aware such shifts are occurring. It's hard to recognize rifts in your inner life when the decibel level of that quiet space is intruded upon so consistently by so much vying to penetrate our thoughts: breaking news, calendar alerts, marketing pitches, work tasks, bank balances, and the numbing titillation of the memosphere—to name but a few of the things the average smartphone alerts us to each morning. And just like that, our connection to the dream space—Harjo's "space not defined or bound by linear time or perception"—is ruptured. Just like that, we begin to lose interest in the part of ourselves that soars beyond the confines of the body, assembling the memories and coaxing the forms of recognition by which we might transcend the limits of everyday logic. The wellspring of hope. The hide-saving tools of intuition and discernment. Even the fortitude to say *No* to what is forced upon us as the best we can expect. Each of these vital capacities is hustled out of reach by the slow scroll, the infinite feed, the myriad converging streams that carry us swiftly toward the urge to be lulled, quelled, distracted.

But our relationship to language has great bearing upon our capacity to be wide awake and at home both in the imperfect world *and* in the dimensions of our full selves. Our ability to ask and grapple with difficult questions. Our willingness to accept uncertainty, to withstand discomfort. The curiosity with which we approach another person's perspective. These things fortify us to recognize and celebrate the complex feelings to which we and others are susceptible. And while engaging with poetry isn't the only way to strengthen our powers of listening and responding, asking and offering, poems are remarkable in their ability to augment our stamina for such tasks. Beyond literature, beyond works of art, poems are acts of attention. Can we attend more rigorously, more compassionately to ourselves and others? Even now, as currents the world over appear to accelerate toward crisis and collision, can we muster the courage to do the indispensable things poems challenge us to do?

To admit the horses. To recognize in them the people we love, and those we struggle to. To accept that each of us has grown splintered over time. To rear up against stalls long trained shut. To nose the grasses that doze or cower in us. To wake and greet the lost, the meek, the bound, the free, the defiant, the terrible, the wild fantastic horses that run even now through your, my, every life.

ANY SMALL THING CAN SAVE YOU
On Grief and Accountability

―

THE FIRST GREAT loss of my life occurred when I was twenty-two, the year my mother's cancer came out of remission to metastasize in her liver and lung. Our family was afforded one full year, give or take, to come to grips with her terminal diagnosis. Of course it wasn't enough. Nothing would have been. Shouldn't she be here still, well into old age, just like her nearly-dozen sisters and brothers? But her path was different. Her work in life, as she professed it, was to tend to the souls of others. She did this in part by reminding her children that we were *wonderfully and fearfully made*, that there was *another world beyond this one*, and that we should strive to *be in this world but not of it*. I console myself now envisioning her busy at work in the universe, though at what I do not know. For my part, her commitment to the purpose of our human existence instilled in me the belief that I occupy a meaningful place in the cosmos. But this present view, which accepts the necessity of her leaving the physical plane, belies my years-long struggle to admit, find language for, and even come to bear a form of appreciation for the role grief has come to play in my life.

For a long time, the shock of impending loss choked me with silence. I didn't talk much about what was happening to my mother. Even in the late stages of her illness, I feared treading too far into any conversation whose terminus was her dying. I worried that acknowledging such an outcome would authorize it, when I believed I ought instead to cleave to the possibility of a miracle, as my mother herself was doing. Most of my conversations skimmed atop the surface of the day-to-day, or swooped back to gather up recollections of times past, where the smallest happy details would swell with something almost like promise. As if talking about them proved that they'd happened, that my mother herself had happened. Bringing the vitality of her living into close range like that, even briefly, was a counterpoint to how far away from us death threatened to sweep her.

Not long after the funeral, I contracted chicken pox. The virus laid me up in a feverish delirium and set my skin, throat, and eyes on fire. I could barely swallow. My mind paced and raged, refusing sleep. But the torment of my body at war against itself supplied a useful container for the grief I bore, the confusion of which had left me feeling marked, gored. I'd spent so much time talking myself back from the notion that my mother's death had befallen *me*. Wasn't it, after all, *her* life unfolding in obedience to *her* destiny? To center my own experience of loss in what I viewed as her story would have been, it seemed to me then, unforgivable vanity. And yet there I was. Unmothered. Unmoored. So for two weeks while the illness ran its course, the temporary abjection of my condition permitted me to rail against a woeful wrong.

I wasn't alone. My entire family grieved. But that's just it: Grief strikes each person differently, employing a unique vocabulary and activating a singular spectrum of feelings for each. Grief drew me into a profound privacy where I'd ponder the person my mother might have understood me to be. Had she guessed at my secrets? Had she forgiven my faults? Had she trusted something in me that I, too, might learn to trust? Mostly I wrestled with the question of who I must go on to be in her absence. Grief, the first cataclysm of my young life, was a tall space filled as if with fog, a place I nevertheless found myself overwhelmingly drawn to, just as my mother's soul, in those final moments of her life, had been drawn up and away from her mortal body. How important it became, in that weightless season, to attempt to gather what it means to live in the *here* to which I was bound, while believing—needing to insist—in the purpose of the *there* to which my mother had disappeared. What else mattered? What else had or would ever come to have the importance of my mother's departure?

Mark Doty's poem "Ararat," which recollects the excitement of a child's first Easter egg hunt alongside the juncture when unbounded possibility gives way to reality, functioned for me at that time as a type of elegy—a poem expressing grief, reverence, and longing for someone who (or something that) has passed into death. Though it contains no mention of traditional bereavement, the poem's turning toward a moment that has been lost to the passage of time, and its movement between happiness and difficulty, made it a useful vehicle for confronting the stations of my own grief.

Ararat

Wrapped in gold foil, in the search
and shouting of Easter Sunday,
it was the ball of the princess,

it was Pharoah's body
sleeping in its golden case.
At the foot of the picket fence,
in grass lank with the morning rain,
it was a Sunday school prize,
silver for second place, gold
for the triumphant little dome
of Ararat, and my sister
took me by the hand and led me
out onto the wide, wet lawn
and showed me to bend into the thick nests
of grass, into the darkest green.
Later I had to give it back,
in exchange for a prize,
though I would rather have kept the egg.
What might have coiled inside it?
Crocuses tight on their clock-springs,
a bird who'd sing himself into an angel
in the highest reaches of the garden,
the morning's flaming arrow?
Any small thing can save you.
Because the golden egg gleamed
in my basket once, though my childhood
became an immense sheet of darkening water
I was Noah, and I was his ark,
and there were two of every animal inside me.

The poem's vocabulary of hope is, at first, unbounded. The prize egg in the speaker's basket, a memory from earliest childhood, might have contained anything. And the poem's means of visualizing that anything—as "the ball of the princess" and "Pharoah's body / sleeping in its golden case"—taps into the magic of fairy tales, and the vanishing point where history becomes indistinguishable from mythology. These opening lines go a long way toward conjuring not just the scope of a single child's hope, but the sense of childhood itself as a state or place in which everything wished for is possible. The tenderness with which the speaker's older sister teaches him to participate in this rite acts as a threshold which the reader, too, is invited to cross:

> my sister
> took me by the hand and led me
> out onto the wide, wet lawn
> and showed me to bend into the thick nests
> of grass, into the darkest green.

But it is a stunted journey. Just as the golden egg is quickly transacted away, so does the magic of the hunt reveal itself to have been only a game. The letdown of this turn of events is underscored by language that brittles from an earlier lushness into something flat and matter-of-fact: "Later I had to give it back / in exchange for a prize."

That's what grief felt like to me. Like my world had been robbed of depth, pounded from three dimensions into two. But as a reader in grief's standstill, "Ararat" helped me to ask, *What do I do now? How am I supposed to go on living after hope and happiness have been taken away?* It didn't matter that no one had died in Doty's poem. In fact, perhaps it was easier for me to ask such bald-faced questions, and remain unfearful of their answers, of a poem in which death is not an overt consideration. And so I took heart in the fact that when the speaker reaches the point in the memory when he has to give the egg back, his impulse is not to narrate further forward in time, but rather to go back again to the beginning and ask, "What might have coiled inside [. . .] ?" In other words, the poem finds ways of prioritizing the past over the present and future, circling back to a moment before hope has given way to knowledge, and before possibility is allowed to harden into fact. Was the egg filled with magic? Any adult reader of the poem has by now come to understand the actual Easter egg as an empty trinket gilded in foil, but the question itself re-imbues the object with potential, attaching it again to the terms once alive in the child's imagination. What the poem really seems to be asking is: *That young self—the self full of light and hope—is he still here?*

There were scenes from my own childhood I replayed for myself during that season of grieving. In one, I sat on the tailgate of our family station wagon beside my mother, picnicking within eyeshot of a pond. A crisp apple diced into tuna salad. Sandwich crusts washed down with lemonade. The silent safety of our togetherness punctuated by birdsong, passing shadows, wind in leaves. Like the Easter egg hunt in Doty's "Ararat," these moments were lost to time, but reconfiguring them in my imagination allowed me to slip momentarily from under the freight of despair. To have once trusted that this was the material of my entire life! To have once been small beside my mother, believing that anything I asked she could answer, anything I needed she could provide! Remembering this—claiming it—offered a consolation so momentous I'd call up this scene and others like it as a counterargument to the freefall of loss. I'd make the momentary choice to be someplace in spirit and imagination, rather than submit to the noplace of despair. This is what Doty's speaker also seems to be turning toward, and what I take him to mean when he asserts, "Any small thing can save you."

Why did I—why do I—read "Ararat" as a kind of elegy? It has to do with more than simply the time in my own life when I first encountered the poem. I discern a familiarity with death coloring images throughout the poem—images drawn into the scene not by the child recollected, but by the adult mind operating in revisitation of childhood, an adult inevitably awake to the many forms of loss a life can contain. I'm thinking of constructions like "body / sleeping in its golden case." Or the descriptors "lank" and "at the foot," which introduce the suggestions of repose and prostration—like Christ's body as rendered in Michelangelo's *Pietà*, say, or the disciples gathered at the foot of the cross in Fra Angelico's *The Crucifixion*. Peppered among the lines leading up to the poem's midpoint, there is even the intimation of a mortal journey: "led me / out onto the wide . . . / and showed me to bend . . . / . . . into the darkest . . ." which seems almost to echo phrases from Psalm 23: "He maketh me to lie down in green pastures: he leadeth me beside the still waters. . . . Yea, though I walk through the valley of the shadow of death . . ." Subtle as these gestures and images are, they have nevertheless been composed into the poem. Like the musical score audible beside or beneath a film's visual narrative, they can be felt to imbue the poem with further ambient tone and emotional texture.

Then, again, the speaker stops time, choosing to turn instead back toward the radical consolation of a once-ago state of belief. As if part of our human reckoning—part of our very survival—has to do with choice. As if a person can choose to survive, can claim or contrive the logic by which surviving makes sense:

> Because the golden egg gleamed
> in my basket once, though my childhood
> became an immense sheet of darkening water
> I was Noah, and I was his ark,
> and there were two of every animal inside me.

Granted, it is a tenuous foothold. See how the poem's consolation is balanced there, following a string of conditions: "because" and "once" and "though." Notice how the "sheet of . . . water" is not *dark* or *darkened* but "darkening" as if childhood itself ended for the speaker before the griefs of that time ceased to accumulate. Yet through all of that and its aftermath, what is capable of buoying him—what he decides to accept as a vital lifeline—is the memory of something he once imagined himself to possess. Not only does the poem's emotional arc quite willfully change direction, but the lifeline itself is speculative, abstract, grounded not in fact, but intention.

In his essay "The Figure a Poem Makes," Robert Frost describes a poem as "a momentary stay against confusion." In other words, though a poem isn't likely to solve or settle everything once and for all, it might offer a glimmer of in-the-moment clarity to the poet, and by extension to the poem's reader. This has little to do with a poet's innate wisdom and much to do with the ways poems are so often motivated by a poet's questions, struggles, and ongoing unrest. *What should I do? Where can I find hope?* Surely there are sanctioned answers to these and other questions that arise in the course of a life, but poetry exists because the sanctioned sometimes fails to console us. And so a poem embarks on a journey of improvisation. This is Frost's description of his own journey of improvisation in the writing of a poem:

> For me the initial delight is in the surprise of remembering something I didn't know I knew. I am in a place, in a situation, as if I had materialized from cloud or risen out of the ground. There is a glad recognition of the long lost and the rest follows. Step by step the wonder of unexpected supply keeps growing.

Frost is describing the ways his own poems lay hold of latent memories and dormant knowledge, and their manner of journeying through recollection, intuition, and imagination, making use of whatever is relevant to the poem's larger conundrum. Frost's metaphor of having "materialized" in a place where he must make use of what he "didn't know [he] knew" tracks with my own sense that moving forward into a poem's unfolding is a matter of paying different forms of attention: to what is present, what is absent, what is seen, felt, wondered. How "step by step" even the patterns at work within language itself begin to bear upon where the poem might arrive, and what forms its clarity might take. For example, when Doty's speaker uses the metaphor of "an immense sheet of darkening water" to describe his childhood, the image brings with it a feeling of depth and threat, of something in which the speaker could drown, or into which he well could have decided to leap. In other words, the element of water makes relevant a new range of associations, which is perhaps one reason why the Sunday school story of Noah's ark, which weathered forty days and nights of punishing flood, becomes relevant or useful to the poem's remembering. Each successive choice opens up certain possibilities for the poet, and at the same time veers away from the usefulness of others. Step by step, choice by choice, the poem continues to unfold until something like realization promises to dawn. The path is seldom straight. This is perhaps the point.

As Frost goes on to remind us, "We enjoy the straight crookedness of a good walking stick."

Oftentimes the revelation of a poem lies in its ability to bend and redirect habitual patterns of thought which insist that the prevailing reality is absolute and immutable. When Doty's poem arrives at a place where suffering asserts itself as a logical point of arrival, the poem stops short, turns back, and asks a new and different question of the past: *Before difficulty sets in, what did I believe myself to hold? Who did I believe myself to be?* This redirection empowers the speaker to stare out at life's dark water, assuring himself that he has long known how to stay afloat.

My own twenty-two-year-old reality lightened and expanded when "Ararat" helped to demonstrate that loss could impart something more than sorrow to my life, and that everything I'd previously held, hoped for, or cherished was mine, still, to claim and to use. There even came a time when I could accept that the loss that had befallen me was in no way unique. I met other daughters whose lives with their mothers had been cut short. I met parents whose children had died. Young men preceded in death by their own young wives. Elderly widows or widowers for whom loss was no more bearable for being expectable. To be drawn back into the world after a period of intense bereavement was, for me, a matter of becoming acquainted with the ways my own suffering connected me to others. The time it takes for loss to sink in. The first morning you wake up not to the shock of remembering that someone you love has died, but knowing this as familiar and incontrovertible fact. Countless others knew and had long known the very same things my mother's death had only recently required me to learn. I was not the only human made to bend beneath mourning, and coming to understand this fact pushed back against the temptation to claim suffering as a thing that set me apart from others, something that gave me permission to expect more than might ordinarily be my due. Because loss is a natural and inevitable function of living. We love fiercely and we are also made to surrender ties that feel as though they ought never to be ruptured. We're all tasked with finding and remaking ourselves in a world riddled with forms of unmaking. Alongside others who lived with such knowledge, I was encouraged to admit that I had lost some but not all of what I cherished, and that even from my position of dearth, I remained equipped to be of support to others.

And doesn't every form of mourning—even the most intimate, the most private-seeming—have bearing upon our relationships to other people? Because grief, at heart, speaks to our grievances with the world. The unfairness of death. The hardship of being forsaken by systems designed to nurture and protect. The injustice of being left to navigate life's nightmares alone. As tempting, as natural as it may feel to insist that having been robbed of something makes you or me someone to whom much is therefore owed, such thinking contrives pain into power, which will eventually demand to be wielded over others.

Frank Bidart's "Curse," written in response to the attacks of September 11, 2001, gives itself over to an outpouring of righteous anger and outrage. As the title suggests, the poem reads as a tirade and condemnation directed at the architects of terror. Here is an excerpt:

> May what you have made descend upon you.
> May the listening ears of your victims   their eyes   their
>
> Breath

enter you, and eat like acid
the bubble of rectitude that allowed you breath.

May their breath now, in eternity, be your breath.

The poem operates as a closed system, in which images like "breath" and "rectitude" occur and recur, passing from victim to aggressor. Built into the form of the poem is the sense that nothing disappears, that everything which enters the world must cycle through again and again. This sense of cycle and recurrence also informs the nature of the curse the poem delivers: *"May their breath now, in eternity, be your breath."* The satisfaction—and the terror—of a poem like this lies in its willingness to rage, to denounce, to level condemnation without filter or fear of judgment. To meet rectitude with rectitude, to descend to the tenor of attack. But I wonder: To what end must a curse obey the directive to repeat? Will a nation that returns violence with violence also be descended upon by the same?

Rereading "Curse" more than twenty years after its initial publication, I'm discomfited to recognize the degree to which the poem's rhetorical strategies fall into step with the most disheartening norms of political discourse to have emerged in recent years. Bidart's speaker, who is so wounded and so angry as to be talking in circles, causes me to wonder: Is our political division the effect of grief, rage, and fear clouding our collective reasoning? "Curse" illuminates to me the ways that violence and the outrage it triggers are means of making us less knowable, and therefore less human, to one another. But if a poem can operate as a space within which to observe, reflect upon, and redirect our patterns of reasoning, then poetry is also a tool for *reconfiguring* our reactions to the pain and loss we experience as a result of the actions of others. The forms of conflict that tip us, in our vulnerability, into patterns of shock and accusation. The fissures that widen into sites of gaping division. The complex upsets that can cause us to go from being neighbors and equals to strangers and adversaries.

I'm thinking of war. How swiftly it is justified, qualified, apologized for as a necessity. And how each of us, knowingly or not, is implicated in some thread of its fabric, which has been spread out across oceans and nations to cover the laps of leaders, of pretenders to power, of citizens and institutions attached by the thinnest of fibers that nevertheless hold tight. What, if we are being honest, does this fact do to our willingness—yours and mine—to reason clearly? We may disagree about the blind spots and fault lines of our shared history—about complicity, and who among us have been deemed inherently innocent or guilty. But having come this far together, Reader, let us not part ways. I'm not suggesting that we retreat into mere civility or decorum—words that have long rattled in power's toolkit for snuffing out the posture of dissent. No, let us instead go, unarmed and open-hearted, into the territory of a poem. . . .

The speaker of Danez Smith's "Rose" looks back on a school-era rivalry. Tit for tat. Defend and attack. It is a kind of war, surely, complete with enemy armies who brandish words as weapons. What does the poem, and the scale upon which it operates, challenge us to recognize about our outrage at harm, and our own complicity in its perpetuation?

rose

we were kindergarten sweethearts. you asked me. i said yes. you were a white girl & not pretty. i liked the shape of your face. it looked like a ball with hair. you were red & puffy. we broke because we were five. it mattered until it didn't. how big a fact at six seven even nine. i treated you like poop. everyone treated you the same. you were the girl with the puffy red face. you were mean. so we were mean. or we were so you. we were nine ten eleven. we were so small & evil. you & barbara sliverman wrapped a jump rope around my neck after i called you a puffy-faced something. when we learned the word bitch, we called you bitch. someone was always willing to remind you of your shit. we were shit, ugly & needed to direct attention everywhere else. girls fought you. said you got around. made you untouchable & easy. you screamed. i remember you always at the top of your lungs. you were kind to your friends. no one liked any of y'all. it was dangerous to be your friend. you were red & dated. your folks shit broke. you were a girl & everyone wanted you to know you were a white frog. if you wished we all watched the last of our water turn to feathers or prayed our children are born with teeth where eyes should be, your prayer was fair. you deserved to parade us through a city of grandmas, smacking ears. if you saw me & stabbed me in the foot i'd understand. we were so mean. i was the bastard fuck in the mob of bastard fucks. the easily swayed torch. o rose, saint of getting roasted in the hallway, warrior queen of the misfits, my love, how did you survive us? if this finds you if there is still a you to find if you know this is about you if you read poems if you take breath into & out of your lungs & find this in a book or in the blue aurora of your phone & this is you: at times i wake in the middle of the night & think

we killed that girl.

One of the first things I notice is the poem's diction, which appears to track quite directly to each age or stage of childhood being recalled. This imparts the feeling that the poem is not just a catalog of reflections, but also something like a field trip to different regions of the past. Accordingly, the first several observations are simple. Friends become "sweethearts" because "you asked me." And "i said yes," because "i liked the shape of your face. it looked like a ball with hair." Being guided into these memories via a juvenile, matter-of-fact form of expression, I'm alerted to how seemingly arbitrary so many of childhood's decisions turn out to be. There is not even much reason behind the breakup of these one-time "sweethearts" other than the fact that they were all of five years old and their affection only "mattered until it didn't."

The first time one of the speaker's actions is attached to logic—"i treated you like poop. everyone treated you the same"—individual accountability is quickly absorbed into and implicitly justified by the actions of the group. Presumably, none of these kids has consciously decided upon a set of norms for their behavior; they've simply been acclimated into an existing culture, accepting things as they are. I wonder if the automatic and unthinking compliance with *things as they are*, which is a large part of what the poem itself seems invested in questioning, may have bearing upon the form Smith has chosen for the poem, for though formal devices operate within a prose poem— similes; metaphors; acceleration and deceleration of pace; an array of tones and vocabularies serving to conjure a crowd of characters over time; and even, toward the end of the poem, silence operating as an emphatic presence—they remain in some ways invisible. Like the invisible norms and expectations beginning to exert pressure on the poem's speaker and the other children in "rose," the reader is guided through the material in such a way as to feel put-upon by the tensions and rivalries of the poem's particular time and place. I feel shoved along as if through a crowded corridor by the blunt, clipped phrases in a passage like "you were mean. so we were mean. or we were so you. we were nine ten eleven. we were so small & evil," which bristles with conflict, airlessness, and something like choicelessness. Even the poem's formatting, printed as it is at a slight angle, like a poster aslant on a wall, or a note askew on a desk, affirms this sense of being crowded into a space, time, and set of arbitrary norms. The repetitions and minor variations in the passage also generate the feeling of acceleration, even as considerations like cause-and-effect or agent and action become blurred. The number sequence "nine ten eleven" adds an awareness of temporality—as if the years are adding up, taking their toll. And look: it is not until age eleven—a whole six years into the poem—that the speaker sees clearly enough to acknowledge "we were . . . evil." The language of moral judgment underscores our recognition that the speaker had a choice, but nevertheless chose wrong. Memory, so often a site of distortion, consents here to being held accountable. But the kindergarteners who opened the poem are by now burgeoning adolescents; see how long such a process has taken?

I wonder if part of what hinders recognition in the poem, and in life, has something to do with the way labels like "good" and "evil" or even "white girl" operate. All labels purport to define people and to help contain situations, steering us toward what and whom has been deemed worthwhile, and away from whom and what hasn't. As a reader of Smith's poem, I can feel myself defaulting to a bevy of received labels in an attempt to pin down the kids in "rose." Are they *rough, reckless, wild*? I can almost hear my late mother pulling me aside to warn, *Those kids are too fast for their own good.* And I'm reminded of how, when I was a high school student in the late 1980s, children of color were beginning to be succinctly pathologized via the word *urban*, regardless of where we lived. Urban Youth, as a label, nullified the individual stories of a wide swath of the population, replacing them with a harmful mythology.

Across human history there have existed terms designed to whittle down the options and lower the ceiling of possibility for people the collective imagination insists are strangers to fortune. *Savages. Barbarians.* People with *the odds against them.* People hailing from *difficult upbringings.* People so routinely associated with minority status that, when two or more are gathered in a classroom or a conference room, they're likely to be mistaken for one another. When they're singled out, their presence might activate an excessive courtesy that only serves to underscore their standing as anomalies. *Charity cases. Diversity hires.* Smith's poem calls attention to the insidious nature of labels by detailing the effects of lobbing Rose with the epithet "bitch," which instantly qualifies her for an onslaught of mistreatment. From this point on, she's fought with, gossiped about, set apart from her peers who, having deflected attention away from themselves, are able to dodge a similar scrutiny. It is as if the label itself is what has made Rose "untouchable & easy." As if having been labeled as such, "bitch" becomes her reality.

It's possible to read "rose" as germane to the confines of a particular experience of childhood. But the feud at the heart of this poem, and the tribalism it describes, make it relevant to any form of conflict in which people are encouraged to choose sides in defense of specific or even symbolic terms of belonging. Group allegiance, while promising a sense of safety and acceptance in community, also functions as a harbor against individual accountability. Perhaps this is why it's taken the poem's adult speaker so long to look back on the relationship in question with an appetite not merely to gawk, but to enact a form of self-scrutiny that summons remorse and humility. What makes such objectivity possible in a poem, when in life it so often eludes us? I suspect the answer may have to do with the ways poems invite us to step into larger, less-constrained, less-observed versions of ourselves and to look closely and unguardedly at things that normally put us on alert. The dissociation, tunnel vision and fight-or-flight of real-life panic cease to apply. We quite literally return to our senses and take things in more deeply, perceptively, allowing empathy and intuition to serve in an act of witness. A poem like "rose," rooted in memory, also brings the capacity of retrospect into play with forms of knowledge and experience that would not have been present at the time in question. Take for instance, the portrait of Rose that occurs just before the poem's midpoint:

> you screamed. i remember you always at the top of your lungs. you were kind to your friends. no one liked any of y'all. it was dangerous to be your friend. you were red & dated. your folks shit broke. you were a girl & everyone wanted you to know you were a white frog.

The brief catalog of observations draws Rose's rage and pain into view. Free of the motivations and defense mechanisms of adolescence, the poem's speaker is empowered to recognize Rose as a person making her way through her own life and the world. And the reader, of course, participates in this exercise in perception. We see Rose literally crying out in crisis. She cries out so much that she stays red-faced from screaming back at the voices and faces telling her she is nothing. Telling her she comes from nothing. This is what it looks like to be mis-seen, mischaracterized, made into fresh kill by a form of predatory fear. This, too, is a portrait of grief. Grief for the self in the process of a merciless undoing.

What revelation, or consolation, does this unflinching portrait yield? It brings the poem's speaker to the point where it is possible to concede wrongdoing and insert into the record the following assessment: "i was the bastard fuck in the mob of bastard fucks. the easily swayed torch." Nothing is asked for. Neither understanding nor forgiveness. The poem's one question is but a further indictment of the speaker's own previous dearth of compassion: "warrior queen of the misfits, my love, how did you survive us?" But the poem continues past penance, and past the seeming largesse of giving one's enemy the final say, in order to allow its speaker to stand accountable: "at times i wake in the middle of the night & think / we killed that girl."

It is in the hush extending from this final line that I ask if a poem like "rose" might lend itself to a consideration of conscience and consequence among larger collectives of people. Beyond cliques of friends, beyond the branches of a family, I wonder how Smith's vision of accountability might speak to something like the social body of a nation. For if poems can bolster us, their readers, through the private travails of grief and mourning, can't they also embolden us to recognize and stand to account for the harms our collective body has ignored or even authorized as appropriate treatment for select persons within or beyond our bounds?

ANOTHER TERMINOLOGY FOR DESCRIBING the mental burden borne by the speaker of Smith's poem—what causes them to "wake in the middle of the night"—is moral injury. In psychology, moral injury describes "the damage done to one's conscience or moral compass when that person perpetrates, witnesses, or fails to prevent acts that transgress one's own moral beliefs, values, or ethical codes of conduct." Heightened collective awareness of post-traumatic stress disorder in veterans of combat has brought a greater attention to other forms of mental and physical harm sustained in the military context. With it has dawned the recognition that all people, regardless of age and background, can experience feelings of moral anguish or unease when their actions, or the actions in which they understand themselves to be implicated, fall into misalignment with their beliefs about what is right and wrong. Aren't we all susceptible to such a condition, given the forms of unintended harm present in so many of life's everyday decisions: What we eat, how we shop, where we live, how we travel from one place to another, whom we prioritize as eligible for our sympathy and support, whom we choose to ignore, and on and on? And if this is the case, what are we to do? Where are we to begin?

The most honest and succinct answer I can offer is, I don't know, and not knowing is a source of fear. I don't believe I'm alone. Fear floods the earth, it seems to me, as a result of so much that we humans, in our appetites and our ingenuity, have sought to wrest away from other sovereign beings: land, water, air, oil, cobalt, lithium, time, gold, market shares, dignity, belief and its sanctity, the ballot and its legitimacy, loyalty, opportunity, autonomy, another's body, credibility, love and its varieties, family, history, hope, fact, space, longevity, silence, happiness, choice, reality. But fear degrades our ability to do anything in the face of what threatens us. Fear stuns, blurs out our options, convinces us it is better to fall silent and still, to consent, to go along and trust that eventually everything will feel normal again. Fear, running its course long enough, convinces us that the moral disequilibrium in which we find ourselves *is* normalcy. Fear dissuades us from believing our bodies, our hearts, our deepest memories. Fear is an isolating, alienating technology. At its most dangerous, fear keeps us from facing or even fully contemplating what, for our own survival, we must endeavor to change.

But a poem can mitigate fear by facilitating a form of dialogue with it. A poem might ask its author, *What wakes you up in the middle of the night? What do you cower from?* And when the poet answers, the poem will likely brighten, inviting: *Sit down here in this chair where you are perfectly safe. Now, let's approach it together.* How do you go toward something in a poem? You approach an aspect of it via thought. Just as a kind of experiment, let's imagine that Danez Smith's poem "rose" emerges from a fear of and concern for the violence saturating American culture. It's a fair guess, given that other poems surrounding this one in Smith's collection *Homie* are invested in state-sanctioned violence against Blacks and other people of color. And so the poem-to-be, seeking to be useful to the full scope of its poet's preoccupation, might sidle up and say, *What if we think about what it means to wage violence? Have you ever hurt anyone? Why? What would you say to them now if you could?* And together the poet and the poem-to-be, which is just an urge, an itch in the mind, will approach the remembered presence of a friend-turned-foe named Rose.

Should you fear a thing more, or less, when you come to accept that you, too, are implicated by it? When, say, your understanding of it grows beyond your own vulnerability, to include the ways you, too, have aided in its perpetuation? I have found that my fear-based helplessness is tempered by an awareness of my own agency. When I manage to learn that it is not distant others alone who are responsible for the things that threaten me. When I am made to see and to feel my own proximity to actions with which I myself disagree. It is then that I can recognize myself as more useful—and more critical—to a problem's solution.

MY OWN SONNET "The United States Welcomes You" emerged from my preoccupation with the prevalence of police violence against unarmed Black citizens in America. Which is to say that the poem extended from a bodily fear, an old deep desire to protect myself and my kind. Is it difficult to understand why? To have been corralled into relation by way of a shared threat is, after all, a prime impetus to insular community. But once I began to see my poem's speaker as vulnerable—at one point in the poem's first draft, he described himself as one among a crowd of others, all standing "hands raised, eyes wide, mute as ghosts"—it became difficult for me to release him to his fate. I refused to invite into my own poem one of the scenes of annihilation that have become almost routinely familiar from so many cell phone videos of Black people dying, and my aversion to conflict was rendering my poem unviable as a work of art. Put differently, my desire to protect my poem's speaker, while correct and in line with my moral desire to protect Black people from being targeted for execution, had steered my poem away from all insight and contradiction. It had rendered it a sermon.

Changing tacks, I decided to invert the poem's form of address, assigning the role of speaker to the apprehending officer. I still held in my mind's eye the image of the detainee standing there in the headlights' glare, hands raised in the air. But he no longer spoke. Having heaved my perspective into that of an imagined police officer,

I understood why: I held a gun in my hands. One trained upon him. I was icy, calm, standing my ground. The authority of law and the precedent of history almost certainly guaranteed me my safety. This new tincture of tension brought unexpected insights, like: Held at gunpoint, you don't even dare plead. You continue for as long as you can to breathe. You cleave to calm, which is to say, life. You watch. You keep alert and ever still. At least I felt in my body—the body I gave over, in mind, to the officer of the law whose mind and voice I sought to believe I could possess—the surety that this deference was what my position commanded. No, the only voice free to roam the bounds of my poem, I understood, was that of the man in command. And so I gave him license to say anything at all—as long as it took the form of a question. (Sometimes a poem needs a constraint. Sometimes the imagination, in order to wander freely, needs to know it is ever so slightly penned in.) This is the poem that resulted from my intentions:

The United States Welcomes You

Why and by whose power were you sent?
What do you see that you may wish to steal?
Why this dancing? Why do your dark bodies
Drink up all the light? What are you demanding
That we feel? Have you stolen something? Then
What is that leaping in your chest? What is
The nature of your mission? Do you seek
To offer a confession? Have you anything to do
With others brought by us to harm? Then
Why are you afraid? And why do you invade

> Our night, hands raised, eyes wide, mute
> As ghosts? Is there something you wish to confess?
> Is this some enigmatic type of test? What if we
> Fail? How and to whom do we address our appeal?

The literal question that is usually posed in real-life situations like these is something like, *Do you know why I stopped you?* or *Where are you headed this evening?* Behind those questions, I intuit others: *What are you doing here? Do you have any idea what you may be in for?* It is as if there in the exchange, beneath the surface of everyday speech, is an understanding that the social order itself is about to be tested. And so my poem opens with a question that seeks to activate that wider range of concern: "Why and by whose power were you sent?" Reading it back to myself, I was reminded of the voices of intergalactic counsels or extraterrestrial rulers in science fiction. And, come to think of it, those degrees of *alienness* felt useful to the psychic distance between the two figures I was envisioning in my poem. The question also set the metrical foot to which the rest of the poem is more or less faithful; the roughly five hard stresses per line helped me know how much to say, and where emphasis should land. It also helped me to anchor the speaker's voice, which is different from my own, to an assurance of authority. He is doing his job as he's authorized to do it. He has the backing of the law behind him.

The next few lines usher into the poem some of the terms of assumption that follow Black people in day-to-day life. Our supposed proclivity for theft. How much we are presumed to dance. How much attention, as both spectacle and threat, the very presence of our bodies in space seems to command. The notion that our laying claim to anything—even something as plentiful as light—is indication that we are somehow out of bounds, taking away a resource from someone more deserving of it. These lines flooded the poem because of the ways that stereotypes so often haunt even the most innocuous interactions between people of different races, let alone one as potentially momentous as being apprehended by the police.

Once, driving from New York to Pennsylvania, I was ushered out of my own vehicle and into the back of a police car parked some long yards away. I had been speeding. The officer cited a law. Something about my California license. For interminable minutes (was it two? five? twenty?) I listened to his radio's garbled voices while he collected two hundred dollars from my financial institution, money the state of Pennsylvania would not trust me to pay at any other time or in any other way. I feared it was a trick. I wanted to keep one foot on the pavement with the door ajar, but it wasn't permitted. My mistrust tempted me to engage him in ordinary chatter, as if he were just a taxi driver, but I kept quiet, knowing better. I sat perfectly still, sipping rapid, shallow breaths. The situation spiked fear in my body, which I worried would mark me as constitutionally guilty. How could I be anything but afraid? I remember how my legs trembled all the way to my waiting vehicle, and for some time after I was back on my way. That sense of being marked by fear is something the speaker of my poem seems to distinguish in or project onto the bearing of the poem's addressee, resulting in a flurry of questions that operate as if to assign guilt: "What is that leaping in your chest?" "Why are you afraid?" "Do you seek / To offer a confession?" "Then / Why are you afraid?" "Is there something you wish to confess?"

There is no mention of a gun in the poem, but you'll see I found a way to use the line, "hands raised, eyes wide, mute as ghosts," in the speaker's address to the suspect in the poem. It's the one moment when I am permitted to linger on the face—the gaze—of the poem's addressee. And in that posture—the posture of a person held at gunpoint—I recognize two kinds of threat. The actual threat of a gun firing upon a person who's body and bearing announce surrender. And the more nebulous threat that enters by way of the collective American Imagination, which trains us to recognize danger in certain people embodying specific profiles. And because I recognize it—because I understand the contorted terms of its logic—have I not, too, somehow absorbed this lesson? That's how I felt writing the poem, inhabiting its speaker and understanding that before us, at the whim of our gun, stood a person deemed responsible for so much in the world no longer staying put the way it used to. It's in this geometry that I understand the speaker's calm is also a manifestation—and a projection, and also a test—of power. A test performed out of the suspicion that, though something in our midst is shifting, the balance hasn't yet been fully decided. This *something*—the poem's site of conundrum—is also the uncertainty with which we in the world live and cope. If the poem's addressee wants to be released without incident, and moreover, if he wants to move forward into a world where the threat of being deemed a worthwhile target for deadly violence has finally lifted, the question is: When and by whose power might such a reality be made manifest?

Every question in every poem is an appeal to all involved: the poem's speaker, its addressee, author, and reader. It does not wait for an answer so much as trust that a query has been raised that might be productively pondered. At the moment when I typed the question "Is this some enigmatic type of test?" I was writing with my ear, writing in obedience to the poem's loose meter and its use of internal rhyme. But realizing that that question made up most of the poem's thirteenth line, I was excited to discover that I was close to having written a sonnet. Was there a turn or a reversal my poem could strive, in its final line, to enact? Looking back at the poem's opening, I recognized in the question, "Why and by whose power were you sent?" the expectation that there may be an authority operating on behalf of the poem's addressee just outside the frame or scope of the poem. But moving forward from there, everything the poem's speaker says seems to suggest that he doubts or is disinclined to respect the legitimacy of this other authority. What if, in the poem's final line, that authority were to return in such a way as to command a wavering of the speaker's certainty? I thought of how people in every walk of life are able to get away with things they know to be wrong. Loopholes, passing the buck, fool's luck. But what about those crucial moments when doubt descends, revealing our plans and schemes to be riddled with vulnerabilities? The poem's last questions—"What if we / Fail? How and to whom do we address our appeal?"—admit the speaker's doubts into the poem. And this glimmer of an opening felt like a productive reversal of course. To further build upon Frost, it affords the figures in the poem a momentary stay against catastrophe.

OF COURSE IT IS not fear alone that hinders us from living in peace with others, or even with ourselves. But fear becomes a means by which we are often coerced into accepting, ignoring, denying, or misidentifying the violence in evidence around us. Fear of offending those we love. Fear of losing what we prize. In situations where it is not language that fails us, but rather we ourselves who fail to claim recourse to adequate or accurate language, poems can challenge us beyond the harbor of silence and abstraction.

I'm thinking of the directness and clarity operating in a poem like Naomi Shihab Nye's "My Wisdom," which unfolds across seventeen very brief sections in observation of everyday life in occupied Palestine. The poem sits within Nye's collection, *The Tiny Journalist*, written in contemplation of Palestinian youth activist Janna Jihad Ayyad, who began posting cell phone videos of human rights protests as a seven-year-old in 2013. The collection doesn't pander to a view of childhood that insists an adult reader will know more or better than the poem's child-speaker; instead, it delivers moments of clarity, or wisdom, by seeing and naming things in ways that leap clear of logical and lexical convention. Here is the third section from the poem:

> Where did the power go?
> Did it enjoy its break?
> Is power exhausted?
> What is real power?
> Who really has power?
> Did the generator break?
> Do we imagine silence
> more powerful because
> it might contain everything?
> Quiet always lives
> inside noise.
> But does it get much done?

In this excerpt, "power" is personified as an "exhausted" someone who needs a "break." My literal mind imagines the electrical blackouts and brownouts that sweep through certain neighborhoods, but I also recognize in the use of the word "power" the astuteness of a child who has grown up under the circumstance of occupation, witnessing the handprint of authority upon the everyday terms of her reality. The insistence of so much repetition in such a short space—"power . . . / . . . break / . . . power . . . / . . . power / . . . power / . . . break"—characterizes the experience of occupation as the state of being acted upon unremittingly by authorized representatives of the occupying power. Powers that seem to flood the speaker's world, wearing themselves out with their granting of this and denying of that, seizing of this and sparing that. So much so, that when the lights go out, she surmises it must be because power is "exhausted." Seen in such a way, occupation becomes a draining, repetitive, degenerative process that invites even a child's skepticism: "What is real power? / Who really has power?" (Because this can't be it.) The answers in circulation have failed to convince her, and so she has sought to become the author of her own wisdom.

Rather than painting her poem's speaker as disillusioned or jaded, Nye endows her with a philosophical largeness of mind. Her world view has not hardened into rigid certainty; it takes the form of question after question. Even the notion of silence holds open the space for an answer grounded not in absence, refusal, or dearth but abundance:

> Do we imagine silence
> more powerful because
> it might contain everything?

My adult mind, from the safety of my own opinions, wants to know who wields silence in the world of this poem. For whom, in the scheme of occupation, is silence a guarantee? I perceive that with its campaigns and justifications, its policing of bodies, language, and thought, power has the tendency to render silence into a tool of control. And while the poem permits me to hold this notion as one example of the "everything" that "silence... might contain," a vocabulary shift in the poem's next gesture redirects my thought process:

> Quiet always lives
> inside noise.
> But does it get much done?

Suddenly the scale of thought in these lines is no longer abstract or absolute; instead, it returns to the terms of the everyday. "Quiet" is neighbor (or tenant) to "noise." And the vastness of "everything" has been replaced with a more graspable "much." Looking back up at the word "power" as it runs through the preceding lines, I can trace its progression from abstract noun to adjective ("more powerful") in the poem. It, too, has become ever so slightly more recognizable as a facet of daily life, which never goes away. Even in the heightened circumstances of political conflict, a person continues to live on the ground, and so the poem draws us back to the scale of the auditory, the tactile, the probable.

Those final gestures also exert additional forms of emphasis. "Quiet always lives / inside noise" feels to me like a gentle challenge: Is it enough to carve out a place of relative peace and safety in a world roiling with the commotion of occupation and war, political instability and civil unrest, wild disparities in health, wealth, safety, and peace of mind? Is it enough to stay "inside" from the noise of the world? Granted, such a decision can be seen as practical. And likewise, as reasonable. One might even argue convincingly that for some, avoiding the fray is responsible. But in the larger scheme of this time in which we live—a time of change and volatility we delicately refer to as one of increasing uncertainty—what is the "much" needing doing, and by what means ought we to be willing to get it done?

These are questions posed mostly to people outside the field of poetry: historians, political experts, scientists, and the like. But our view of reality dwells in patterns of thought and expectation that reside in language. What we tell ourselves when we're afraid or angry, or when we're shocked into outrage or silence—even then, it is language, via thought, that operates to assure or embolden: *She never listens. He isn't telling the truth. I don't know what to do. It's okay, we'll be safe.* Therefore, to create new patterns of language, as poems and poets exist to do, is to alter or correct course on our story of reality. To move from a state of fear to one of understanding, or from the sense that you are small and bound by the circumstances in your life to an acknowledgement that you are large and your purpose eternal—that kind of transformation begins in language, in talking and listening to yourself, to others, to a voice on a page. Language is the engine for our sense of the possible, and poetry fosters a productive impatience with the notion that things as they are cannot or must not be made to change.

WHO ARE YOU?

On Strangers and Others

I'VE WRITTEN ELSEWHERE about the experience of my first encounter with the poet Emily Dickinson. I was eleven years old and in the fifth grade when I happened upon one of her widely anthologized short poems in a schoolbook:

> I'm Nobody! Who Are You?
> Are you—Nobody—too?
> Then there's a pair of us!
> Don't tell! they'd advertise—you know!
>
> How dreary—to be—Somebody!
> How public—like a Frog—
> To tell one's name—the livelong June—
> To an admiring Bog!

The voice on the page, from the many dashes and exclamations, seemed breathless, as if the speaker had hurried across some distance to catch me up in her excitement. Under these circumstances, the word "Nobody" struck me as different than I had understood it up to that point. It wasn't an absence of presence, not a dearth of importance, not even an error or a false impression—the way a telephone or doorbell might seem to ring, though when you go to answer it, nobody's there. No, Dickinson's Nobody felt rich with character and spirit, like the kind of friend I most longed to meet, who could teach me to see whole worlds in empty spaces and hear music in what passed for silence. She knew all about me. She seemed to want to claim me. Why else would she have gone to such trouble to catch me alone, and to assure me that we two were something as special as "a pair"?

I felt the power of words like "dreary" and "livelong" in the second stanza, words I seldom myself used. Dreary was a word that signaled the particular gloom of boredom. Things are dreary to children who have what they need, but for whatever reason lack what they want. On dreary days in my own home, I was often told to sit and read or entertain myself at an otherwise quiet task. But "livelong" conjured ardor, the exhaustion of being too busy, and at something too burdensome. One of the only places I'd heard that word before was in a song we kids were often encouraged to sing: "I've been working on the railroad / All the livelong day!" A song about day-in-day-out drudgery, sung by a character whose sole dream of reprieve is that someone will blow the whistle signaling the end of the current work shift:

> Dinah, won't you blow,
> Dinah, won't you blow,
> Dinah, won't you blow your horn?

"I've Been Working on the Railroad," like other popular children's songs from my childhood, has its origins in minstrelsy, a form of entertainment created to assure white audiences that Black people were little more than children. Gullible. Disinclined to work. Wanting nothing but to loaf and joke, sing and play. In the framework of nineteenth and early twentieth century minstrelsy, Blacks were routinely characterized in ways that downplayed the injustice of slavery and the convict leasing system. Instead, these tunes enforced the impression that Blacks sang and fooled, beholding their lot in life, before and after emancipation, not as brutal or unjust, but merely *dreary*. By this same distorted characterization, when they weren't shucking or bucking duty, Blacks were making popular entertainment out of their own despair. Minstrelsy as an art form originated to reinforce and codify the notion that Black people, economic pawns, were nobodies—inconsequential, unworthy of empathy or genuine regard, like the speaker in yet another popular minstrel song, who sings over and over again, "Oh, Susanna, don't you cry for me—"*

The legacy of racial caricature has given birth to unshakable stereotypes about Blackness. How we Blacks are presumed to look, to feel, to act. What it is assumed that we want. The means to which we will go in order to get what we crave and avoid what we have coming. The weight of these stereotypes upon my life as a child in the 1970s and '80s surely had bearing upon what made the paradox of Dickinson's Nobodyness so compelling to me, because it affirmed the depth and discernment a quiet part of myself knew I possessed. To stand alone, or be willing to. To revel, confident, in an unadvertised complexity. And to know enough to guard such capacities as precious.

These assurances—I'd heard them before from my parents—

---

* Other examples of minstrel songs still routinely sung in American public schools in the late twentieth century are "Camptown Races," "Jimmy Crack Corn," and "Old Dan Tucker."

became ever more appealing because of the way they operated alongside the images in Dickinson's poem. Suddenly, the popular people, the institutions authorized to judge me, and even the part of me that sometimes felt willing to become less myself in order to fit in with those and other sites of longing—suddenly all of that became the league of frogs belching and bellowing out from the depths of a cold bog. The slick glabrous skin, the viscous murk of those overgrown waters, the desperate incessant crooning and croaking. Confronting such a scene in all its sensory detail, you don't seek to parse the nuances of gain and loss, integrity and compromise; quickly and decisively, you react: *If that murky mess is full of Somebodies, I'd rather be Nobody!*

Of course, it's more than that, too, isn't it? Because the power to invite or exclude, condemn or anoint is also, quite literally, about *power*, to which not all—relatively few, in fact—are granted access. I wasn't. Neither were my parents, though their authority was understood to be absolute in our household. I didn't know anything about Dickinson when her poem first held me in thrall, but even she, born into an elite nineteenth-century family, was frustrated by the manifold barriers to validation she faced as a woman seeking to publish her poetry. And yet, her poem's rebuke to systems of validation that fail to recognize certain of us, or to see us correctly, came through. The people who snub, judge, and expect the worst of us. The feeling of being sized up and passed over. It made sense that Dickinson's Nobodyness was a refusal to accept diminishment, a way of saying, *I draw my authority from within.* And like the Black folk humor I'd been exposed to, which used laughter to poke holes in the presumed authority of our detractors, Dickinson's poem even dished out its rebuke with a dollop of humor, attaching a word like "public"—the awareness of which usually puts a person in the crosshairs of considerable judgment and scrutiny—to something as low-down and unimposing as "a Frog." Likewise, the poem's sonic closure hinges upon a similar dressing down of external admiration—something common wisdom insists we must endeavor to earn—by anchoring it to (or submerging it within) the depths (and blunt direct rhyme) of a "Bog!"

Yet there's more still, isn't there? Because those assurances I'd grown up hearing from my parents—the reminders that I was wonderful and capable, unique in all the world—were given to me most fervently in moments when my young self needed to be built back up after having suffered the heartache of being mis-seen or excluded altogether. Perhaps Dickinson's poem is an earnest attempt, on behalf of the poet or an imagined someone, to build herself back up from a moment of disillusionment or doubt. After all, a large part of the consolation of poetry as an art form stems from the fact that poems emerge not from what poets have already mastered, but from the lessons and realizations they are compelled to reckon and struggle with—sometimes over and over again throughout the span of a life. And that struggle doesn't happen completely off-site; poems themselves are artifacts of an artist's reckoning, a roadmap to the shifts, leaps, and redirections of attention that have given way to momentary insight, clarity, and unburdening.

Take Dickinson's long dashes. What if they are sparks of something more complicated than acceleration or alacrity? What if they are the kinds of pauses—like deep steadying breaths—a person might take before stepping further into the risk of unabashed honesty? What if here and elsewhere in her body of work, we were to read Dickinson's signature punctuation as indicative of junctures where nonverbal cues can be felt to break in, bearing witness to circumstances that *do* manage to unsteady the speaker? What if each dash marks some new measure of resolve to keep moving forward into a forthrightness neither commonplace nor wholly advisable in everyday circumstances? Dickinson's very punctuation may be indication that hers is a hard-won composure, and one easily ruptured. Hence the poem's one warning: "Don't tell! they'd advertise—you know!" As if the ultimate punishment for the peace of hard-won self-assurance would be to see it intruded upon and nullified by the horde. And what does the dash preceding "you know!" challenge the reader to acknowledge? Perhaps, simply and profoundly, that we *do* know how ruthless and punishing the world can sometimes feel. And we do, don't we? In another of Dickinson's versions of the poem, the line reads, "Don't tell! they'd banish us—you know!" How do you banish nobodies? Perhaps you pull them away from themselves, from their grounding in their own inner authority?

A poem can also call attention to what it feels like to be misseen or wrongly characterized. The ease with which an external gaze, bringing with it conscious and unconscious motives and expectations, can enact a form of erasure upon its subject is spotlighted in Victoria Adukwei Bulley's poem "The Ultra-Black Fish":

The Ultra-Black Fish

Two hundred metres down, the light stops.
Many deep-sea creatures alive at this level
of the ocean have developed the ability to create
light for themselves. This is known as bioluminescence.
Others, on the contrary, contribute to the darkness

by adding themselves to it. Ultra-black fish are
one example, & in 2020 sixteen varieties of these were
~~discovered~~ captured. The level of pigment in their
skin was so high that it was found to absorb 99.956%
of the light that touched it. Karen, a marine biologist,
~~made the discovery~~ came upon them by accident.
Instead of hauling up the deep-sea crabs she had been
searching for, her net produced a fang-toothed fish that
wouldn't show up in a photograph. Held, later, in a tank
under two strobe lights, the fish became a living black hole,
with no discernible features beyond the opacity of its
silhouette. As though it had cut itself out of the image & left.
Scientists believe that the fish developed their invisibility
to aid them in escaping their predators. Another theory
suggests that the obscurity of ultra-black fish enables them
to more successfully catch their prey. It is likely that both
ideas are true. Commentators ~~on their discovery~~ have also
speculated that the chemical structure of the pigment could serve
the development of military & defence technologies.
Nothing was said, however, about how ultra-black fish find
& enter into relations with each other. Nonetheless, their existence
alone is evidence that, invisible as they may be to others,
they are by no means strangers to themselves.

"The Ultra-Black Fish" is a found poem* compiled almost entirely of journalistic coverage of research conducted in the summer

---

* Found poetry is a practice of reworking or reformulating an existing text or texts, with the intention of locating and facilitating new forms of meaning and awareness.

of 2020 by a US-based marine biologist. But gestures within the poem also resonate subtly or emphatically with events from that same summer of global racial uprising following the deaths of George Floyd, Ahmaud Arbery, and Breonna Taylor, including debate around the value of Black lives; and various confrontations in which white women deemed "Karens" were caught in cell phone videos challenging the rights of Black citizens to be present in public parks, in front of their own homes, or elsewhere in space and time. Part of what this poem invites the reader to discern is the degree to which Blackness has been associated, in the public imagination, with chaos, intrusion, and threat. With its strikethroughs and corrections, and via its articulation of unasked questions and logic the popular imagination has failed to ponder, the poem also offers a correction or recalibration of these deeply ingrained habits of perception.

If every poem enacts a literal plunge or descent from the title, which sets up questions and expectations in the reader's mind, down into the body of the poem, where those first inklings will be affirmed or redirected, the first line of "The Ultra-Black Fish" delivers us to a place that is alien and inhospitable: "Two hundred metres down, the light stops." That verb—"stops"—furthers the impression that we have gone too far. It's not that the light dwindles to nothing, nor that it fails to penetrate this depth, but rather that, as if out of its own better judgment, it has put on the brakes. This sense of danger persists, as I see it, via the use of the word "alive" in line two (which bears the shadow of its opposite, *dead*), as opposed to, say, "living" (which brings with it the active possibility of *thriving*). Nevertheless, the creatures operating at this depth have evolved tactics of survival. They "create / light for themselves," or else they "contribute to the darkness / by adding themselves to it." How do these phrases further inform my experience of the poem? For one thing, they impart an aura of moral judgment, with their stark distinction between the "light" and the "darkness" and the impression that all life at this depth is forced to choose sides between one force or the other. I'd even say that the color field of black—in the species name "ultra-black fish" and a statement like "the level of pigment in their / skin was so high"—activates a reader's awareness of race. (To claim not to notice this coincidence might be a matter of going out of one's way in order not to see color.)

Gradually, the poem's spotlight shifts from the anomalies of the ultra-black fish to the scrutiny to which the species is subjected, and the authority "Karen, a marine biologist," is afforded in her role. As a corrective to this historical pattern of granting white interlopers the authority to intrude into Black life, foreign or external agency in the poem is dialed back via strikethroughs: "in 2020 sixteen varieties of these were / ~~discovered~~ captured" and "Karen [. . .] ~~made the discovery~~ came upon them by accident." The strikethroughs insist that a reader recognize and process the intervention that has occurred. As the poem makes this case, it also invites the reader to recognize the distinct vocabularies that have been attached to Blackness and whiteness, not merely in this poem, but in everyday life. One is stark, dire, riddled with terms of noncompliance and predation—such as "wouldn't show up," "a living black hole, / with no discernible features," "cut [. . .] out [. . .] & left," "escaping their predators," and "catch their prey," while the other, which is visible despite redaction, is calibrated to assert dominion, discernment, and expertise. The poem, up until this point, resonates as uncanny not because Bulley has labored to plant these details where they do not exist, but rather because she has happened upon evidence of these patterns of perception, power, and permission in the darkness of the deep sea, where we wouldn't have expected them to be replicated.

The moment when a poem leaps free of its established patterns is exciting, because such a gesture is so often a gateway to unexpected feeling, observation, and discovery. The most breathtaking moment in Bulley's poem comes, for me, after the terms of argument have been elaborated—just at the juncture where a new vocabulary enters in. Bulley has said that, apart from the few "corrections" to text that has been struck through, the only non-found text in her poem occurs in the final four lines:

> Nothing was said, however, about how ultra-black fish find
> & enter into relations with each other. Nonetheless, their
>   existence
> alone is evidence that, invisible as they may be to others,
> they are by no means strangers to themselves.

Beyond evidence, beyond further illustration, what this shift brings into the poem is an alternate vocabulary of perception. We are led into a rich, mysterious "Nothing" that defies the lexicons enforced by habit. That "Nothing," like the vast overwhelming expanse of the sea, includes all that has not been seen, all that has eluded capture. It is the place where any and everything is yet possible. I take it as an invitation to stretch beyond the by-now-familiar terms that have played out in the poem—in the poem and upon the earth. What would it look like to envision—or wait to be shown—the dynamics of relation, care, and self-making that are possible, even preferable, for those who have been held in the most constrictive regions of the global imagination? We are not any longer talking about fish, are we? We're being invited to imagine what liberation of the imagination might look and feel like, and to consider what would be possible—for everyone—were we to but swim beyond the predictable dynamic of power and subordination. And in the slow meanwhile, as we wait and work to unlearn old patterns of scrutiny, there's consolation in the poem's assurance that members of the scrutinized species of the poem are well-equipped to recognize and receive one another ("Then there's a pair of us!"). Inscrutable to most, they, like the myriad Nobodies in our midst, "are by no means strangers to themselves."

ERASURE IN POETRY IS a method of deliberately redacting an existing text in order to uncover alternate meanings. It is a means of making visible that which lies buried within the field of a familiar text. But that's only part of the undertaking. By a further tilt of the imagination, the practice of erasure asks us to conceive of that which remains as-yet-unimagined in the field of what passes for common reality—that which we have mistaken, in our haste or our arrogance, for "Nothing" and for "Nobody." In inviting readers to look more closely at, or listen more intently to, what has been overlooked, taken for granted, or accepted without question, erasure is a way of countering the everyday negations that render people—all of them unique and essential on the human plane—insignificant in the scheme of power. The redaction of an existing text unburies unexpected testimony and delivers it to those whose experience it affirms or corroborates, while also making it legible—even undeniable—to those who don't operate at the frequency of Nobodyness and to whom it may therefore be news. The challenge of writing a poem in this way is to listen to or with the given text while remaining free of a predetermined agenda—to allow the text itself to alert you to fresh insights, useful counterpoints, and uncanny parallels. As a writer who has worked in this very mode, I always tell myself that if I approach the originating text looking merely to criticize or dress down its author or originally intended audience, I'll discover nothing but my own ego (balanced, as it were, atop its high horse), and the poem will fail. But if I can go gently, attentively, and trust that language and time can work together to unburden any text from the original intent for which it may have been written, then I might trust that other forms of clarity can be liberated to reveal themselves.

In April 2017, I attempted an erasure of the United States Declaration of Independence, coauthored by Thomas Jefferson, Benjamin Franklin, John Adams, Roger Sherman, and Robert R. Livingston, and originally published on July 4, 1776. I was looking for otherworldly help in reviving a poem I had previously written and published in contemplation of Jefferson. Something about that earlier poem continued to befuddle me. I felt myself to be talking only toward my own notion of Jefferson. That poem had not yet managed to reach or even fully to believe in Jefferson as an entity alive in spirit or mind and perhaps even still pondering his own life's work. And so I figured that listening to some relic of his voice might allow a fuller form of contact to occur. If that unsettled me as a spooky proposition (it did, slightly), I assured myself that though opinions differ as to what documents such as the US Constitution and the Declaration of Independence *intend*, the collective American Imagination insists that the Founding Fathers live on, through these, their *living* documents.

The first thing I noticed was that, though I'd been made to read the Declaration of Independence in school, I'd never opened myself up to it in the way listening for some scrap of Jefferson's voice, and with it his personal message to *me*, required me to do. In other words, it had never before occurred to me to read that public document with the openness and emotional availability with which I would approach a poem. For to enter into an encounter with a poem you are reading, or a poem you are endeavoring to write, and to be met there by the unwavering attention of a voice that has rushed across all manner of space and time to reach and entreat you, is to be invited to believe, even briefly, that you are unique and irreplaceable in the universe. And what if the voice that reaches you—like Jefferson's on its path that day to me—belongs to someone who, in their own lifetime, may never have chosen or even deigned to address you in such a way? And what if I were to insist that it felt as though Jefferson and I were facing one another not as strangers, nor as adversaries, but as coevals, two souls sparked at the same instant from Eternity? What forms of reparation—between living people, and between people and their living institutions—might be enabled by a voice, caught at just the right angle, on a page?

My own poem "Declaration," written—or, it seemed, rather, *deciphered*—swiftly on that April day, relates what Jefferson seemed to emphasize to me as his rapt audience of one:

Declaration

He has

> *sent hither swarms of Officers to harass our people*

He has plundered our—

> *ravaged our—*

>> *destroyed the lives of our—*

taking away our—

> *abolishing our most valuable—*

and altering fundamentally the Forms of our—

In every stage of these Oppressions We have Petitioned for Redress in the most humble terms:

> *Our repeated Petitions have been answered only by repeated injury.*

We have reminded them of the circumstances of our emigration and settlement here.

> *—taken Captive*
>> *on the high Seas*
>>> *to bear—*

What animates "Declaration" is a willingness, on the part of one of the text's original authors, to lend this appeal for freedom from an unjust colonial authority to me, and with me, my entire race. *This is what you seek*, Jefferson seemed to say. Or, *This is what you need to see.* I was moved to find such direct parallels between the document's cited grievances against the government of England and generations of Black people's pleas to this country for freedom and a full portion of citizenship and justice. As I see them, each of the dashes in my poem opens onto a surging sea of examples. One line that startled me as the poem was being composed is *"and altering fundamentally the Forms of our—"* which my ear involuntarily completed with "families." But the dash also insists that there is always another answer, another layer of evidence and possibility, willing to lend itself to each of these gestures. I hope it also invites the reader to populate the poem's silences (that is, its redactions) with their own understanding of what is withheld. Once, at a reading in Washington, DC, an audience member told me that the poem's final silence, in her ear, contains the word *witness*. She activated a possibility that had not previously occurred to me. I had been thinking about the weight—what I often refer to as the *freight*—of history. Both are compelling to me, and neither should be made to foreclose upon the many other valid terms of hope, loss, need, and deservingness to which the poem lends credence.

Rhythm, emphasis, silence. Inflection, mystery, candor. Flashes of insistence. Irreducible complexity. These things, and others besides, are tools by which poems seek us out in the fullness of our humanity: selves unperturbed and undiminished by the pressures, dismissals, and vicissitudes of power and normativity. But I think there is more operating as well, though I can never prove it. I believe that an equation must exist in which *Language + Time = Clarity*. The unburdening of any text from the rigidity of its original purpose or intention. And so Jefferson, wherever and whatever he now is (perhaps a soul in a different kind of life, or a form of energy at work in the universe) is able to see the larger or farther-flung truths to which his own once-ago voice might now be freed to apply. Accordingly, his words drift forward, reconfiguring themselves to be of use to new purposes. If it is possible even simply to imagine that such a form of regard exists, should it not have some bearing upon what we might be allowed to expect for and from ourselves? By which I mean: We whom habit and custom have rendered Nobodies, and you who have been counted among the sons and daughters of this nation's never-gone Fathers, must come to accept that all of us, together, inhabit and are responsible for the co-creation of a common reality. What will we make of it?

If there really is such a thing as common reality, something we move through each day beside others as actual as ourselves, then what causes so many to doubt—to need to doubt—that circumstances real for some are ones to which they themselves are, or might one day become, susceptible?

Back in grade school, my classmates and I were made to sing together, each standing at our desks during music class. One traditional spiritual, "Oh, Sinner Man," was new to me, but I recognized in the words and the way they were sung that they had something to do with me, my family, and the generations of our people who had endured the experience of slavery—

Oh, sinner man, where you gonna run to?
All on that day.

In the song's narrative, the sinner man first runs to the sea, but the sea is "a-boiling." He runs to the rocks, but they're soon to be "a-melting." He runs finally to the Lord, but the time for repentance has passed and he finds himself refused yet again. We listened and sang along to the record our teacher would play on a turntable wheeled into the classroom atop a cart. Some boys (were all or just most of them white?) did their best to drop their voices down to the low bass baritone of the men (whom I reckoned to be Black) singing on the album's track. The boys lifted their shoulders and dropped their chins, trying to reach a place of depth in their own spindly bodies. They smirked and grinned, abandoning composure. The song struck them as a joke. Of course it would have. America seemed to reserve a different question for many of them, one with loopholes and workarounds, privilege that applied to them, but not to all. That's the gist of what I surmised. I knew—we all knew—it wasn't nice, or right, only that the thing had long ago been decided. Sometimes, when something wrong had been said or done to me or someone like me, I'd catch the glint of this knowledge in another kid's eyes, followed by little more than a quick shrug of the shoulders. Their share of a collective contrition. Before the whole episode was brushed aside, someone might utter a version of the phrase, *It's just the way things are*. I suppose the logic went, or goes, that if no Somebody felt attached to the wrong, then the wounded—a Nobody—was expected not to admit the brunt of the blow.

This doubt—this *need to doubt*—that circumstances real, say, for me are ones to which you, too, might be susceptible. This refusal to accept that, though different, we are siblings and equals. It is an old stance. I discern it again lately in the tumult of frustration resulting from the many current calls for justice for all, frustration that has mobilized into adamant counter calls: *Take America Back! Make America Great Again!* Meaning: *Your justice—your America—your history—your reality—does not and never will apply to me.* No, in America it's true that, subtly or not, we've long been taught (the message comes from many sides) that there's no such thing as common reality. That if it exists, it's only for some. See how, already, the notion—*common* reality—has been marked, marred by a lower sort? Handouts, giveaways, grimy bodies struggling as if up a hill, over a wall, to take what they don't deserve. But if it is ours, can't we will common reality, which many fear as cramped and dim, into a space with infinite dimensions?

In her prose poem "We Are Not Responsible," Harryette Mullen uses the language of the institutional disclaimer—those warnings and liability limits we've grown used to hearing from airlines, restaurants, pharmaceutical companies, insurance providers, law enforcement agencies, and elsewhere—to tap into the assumptions and fears underlying the limits placed upon one person's obligation to another and, by extension, on a nation's duty to its citizens:

We Are Not Responsible

We are not responsible for your lost or stolen relatives. We cannot guarantee your safety if you disobey our instructions. We do not endorse the causes or claims of people begging for handouts. We reserve the right to refuse service to anyone. Your ticket does not guarantee that we will honor your reservations. In order to facilitate our procedures, please limit your carrying on. Before taking off, please extinguish all smoldering resentments. If you cannot understand English, you will be moved out of the way. In the event of a loss, you'd better look out for yourself. Your insurance was cancelled because we can no longer handle your frightful claims. Our handlers lost your luggage and we are unable to find the key to your legal case. You were detained for interrogation because you fit the profile. You are not presumed to be innocent if the police have reason to suspect you are carrying a concealed wallet. It's not our fault you were born wearing a gang color. It is not our obligation to inform you of your rights. Step aside, please, while our officer inspects your bad attitude. You have no rights we are bound to respect. Please remain calm, or we can't be held responsible for what happens to you.

Because it nods to English as a dominant language, and references the murder of twenty-three-year-old Amadou Diallo (who, standing outside his home in 1999, was fired upon forty-one times by police officers who took him for a suspect and assumed that the wallet he sought to remove from his pocket was a firearm), it is reasonable to imagine that the poem's setting is the United States. But national identity becomes less essential a compass than the prevailing dynamics of authority and submission, power and coercion in which the poem's populations—its "We" and "You"—are bound.

"We," the poem's first-person plural speaker, sees itself as belonging to a favored class, one holding the reins of authority. The poem's addressee, a second-person plural "You," is barked at roughly.

"We" is not obligated to hear or recognize "You" in their pleas, nor is "We" liable to believe anything "You" states as truth. Any welcome that "You" may have once been extended—any permission to be present in space and time—is provisional; in fact, the poem's tone suggests that welcome has long since been revoked. Moreover, what "You" seems to seek—protection, redress, regard—is deemed out of line, a bridge too far. From the degree of authority claimed by the poem's "We," the pronoun may well represent a government charged with the care of its citizens and which, in turn, demands adherence to specific terms of compliance. But there are moments when "We" might just as easily be a group of individuals considering themselves the *rightful* citizens of a place: those born within its borders of parents similarly documented, or those with wealth and social standing, or simply those with specific traits who, for these or other reasons, claim and are afforded a privileged standing. In fact, the ambiguity surrounding this "We" is useful. Its amplitude urges me to remain mindful of the ways that the "We" of central authority is always a thing-in-motion. In defending what they believe themselves entitled to, an array of distinct individuals may choose to align themselves, even if only rhetorically, with the dominant "We." For example, when I encounter "We are not responsible for your lost or stolen relatives" in the poem's opening sentence, I recall certain discussions in which people I've known have sought to deflect accountability for the sins of history (*But I didn't own slaves! I can't be expected to pay for the crime of slavery!*) or to distance themselves from what they view as the shame of involuntary subordination (*I wouldn't have been a slave! I'd have whupped Massa's ass!*). Equally decipherable in the same line is the passionless voice of a civil servant seeking to absolve the office he represents of its obligation to account for individuals lost track of in the various channels of a massive bureaucracy: war, asylum, incarceration, forced relocation, and yes, even the still-churning wake of slavery. From moment to moment in the poem, "We" can be seen to accommodate one or another person seizing the opportunity to put the "You" against whom they struggle and the "We" to whom they themselves belong (or seek to) in their rightful (or wishful) places.

Of course, "You" is also a moving target in the poem, one characterized by the poem's "We" as a needy, demanding presence "begging for handouts" and raising "frightful claims." But who is "You," really? In my readerly imagination, "You" descends from generations of people considered to be out of place and in the way. People seeking refuge. People hustling to keep up, sweating to get ahead, hounded by the doubts and suspicions of the American Imagination. People to whom the doors of opportunity have remained shut, and for whom the threat of punishment remains disproportionately high. And like their "lost and stolen" relatives, the poem's "You" is also denied adequate routes of redress: "You are not presumed to be innocent." "It is not our obligation to inform you of your rights." It is as if "You" moves and lives in a system designed to hold them in place or move them "out of the way" rather than to facilitate their advancing to the ranks of "We." Formally, the poem's prose block even suggests a closed system—one with rigid and inflexible bounds that refuses even to accommodate certain words ("cannot," "handouts," "resentments," and "luggage") without breaking them. "We Are Not Responsible" has been widely reproduced online as a lineated five-stanza poem. In such a form, the poem's many end-stopped lines and stanzas, which are slowed down or arrested by terminal punctuation, serve to wordlessly underscore the fact that every office of appeal is shuttered; every potential offramp from this system's gridlock is actually a holding pattern, a dead end for the poem's "You."

"You" is, of course, a Nobody.

No matter the position you or I might be accustomed to in life, as readers we are invited to roam and respond to the full expanse of the poem. In doing so, we're made to cross divides we've otherwise been taught or warned to respect. Unsettlingly, we are put in the position of being barked at as "You" throughout the poem, while also participating in the reification of a rigid and unapologetic "We." Accordingly, I feel impatience—even outrage—rising like a form of memory in my cells when, four sentences into the poem, gestures of expectation and admonishment collide:

> Your ticket does not guarantee that we will honor your reservations. In order to facilitate our procedures, please limit your carrying on. Before taking off, please extinguish all smoldering resentments.

But I know the drill. It will get me nowhere to make a fuss, much less a stink. In this state of emotional clench, I'm nevertheless startled when the last word in each of these three sentences swerves to enact a rapid raising of the stakes. Where my ear, habituated to familiar disclaimers, had been expecting the word *reservation*, the appearance of "reservations" puts me in mind of moral hesitation resulting from differing value systems. While "carrying on" nods to carry-on luggage requirements, the phrase is actually addressing itself to deviations from expected norms of behavior. I'm reminded of the ways that racial "others" are often scrutinized in predominantly white spaces, scolded for making ourselves too visible, too audible, for failing to blend in. And of the occasions when our hesitations in the face of a brusque authority are brushed off, our doubts turned back on us as signs of our own derangement: *You act like you think the world is out to get you....* The poem's many disclaimers work together to remind me that social norms enforcing the silence and blending-in of minorities exist for the comfort of the dominant population, who wish not to be bothered by carryings on of dissent, critique, or demands for redress. The final sentence in the excerpt calls my attention to long-standing upsets that remain unresolved; like a cigarette that hasn't been fully tamped out, old griefs continue to fill the poem's common air with their reek.

Each time I revisit this poem, I am met by a frightening recognition of the expediency with which the fullness and complexity of a whole person can be flattened into something as dimensionless and as futureless as *threat, target, nuisance, suspect*—assumptions resorted to even in the absence of evidence, and which, over time, the American Imagination has come to authorize and even sometimes encourage. And I'm reminded that the biases distorting a culture's view of certain groups of people almost always begin in language: *Affirmative Action takes opportunities away from white people and gives them to underqualified minorities*; *Black men are dangerous*; *Border Control must deter bad hombres down there from coming up here*. And—like a song we've been mis-hearing for years—gradually these distortions begin to ring too familiar not to be somehow credible: "We do not endorse the causes or claims of people begging for handouts," "You were detained for interrogation because you fit the profile," "It's not our fault you were born wearing a gang color." This is precisely the point. It's a vicious cycle, a downward spiral. Our familiarity with distortions of logic makes us increasingly comfortable with, and susceptible to, misleading or deliberately false language. The end game is harrowing: To allow one's thoughts to be habituated to ready-made phrases, deliberate falsehoods, and the like is to become increasingly vulnerable to the tactics of authoritarianism. As George Orwell writes, "Political language—and with variations this is true of all political parties, from Conservatives to Anarchists—is designed to make lies sound truthful and murder respectable, and to give an appearance of solidity to pure wind." Mullen's poem places readers on the discomfiting receiving end of lies and "pure wind." More than that, it urges us to reckon with the annihilating tempest this wind, over time, adds up to.

The poem's final disclaimer—"Please remain calm, or we can't be held responsible / for what happens to you"—creates a gaping loophole through which "We" can dodge accountability for any harm incurred by, or leveled against, the entire group or class addressed as "You." To see the phrase "for what happens to you" there on its own at the end of the poem, severed from any agent whatsoever, is frightening—as if all of the poem's energy, and all of its accrued momentum, have been driving toward this one dark promise. Reading the poem just over two decades after its initial publication, I find myself alerted to events still fresh in public memory, like the 2015 death of twenty-five-year-old Freddie Gray, who suffered fatal spine injuries while riding alone, handcuffed and shackled, in the back of a Baltimore police van.

What does it mean that I can maintain my bearings in a poem that frames and addresses me as if I am a burden and a threat? Perhaps, simply, that the poem seems to exist and operate within the world I recognize. A world in which the circumstance that pits

Somebodies against Nobodies, "We" against "You," is not innate hatred, not inborn rancor, not even flagrant or intractable animosity, but simply custom. The poem's many verbal violences—its indications of mistrust, its deflections of responsibility and its threats of punishment—are merely the strategies by which resources like wealth and social capital have customarily been maintained and defended. Strategies born of the belief that the value of these things is predicated upon their scarcity, and that the peace of mind they bring should therefore be reserved for the exclusive benefit of the elect few: the poem's, and the world's, "We."

But where the default terms of common reality have been calibrated to the ego's demand to stand above others, poetry, which takes the form of an intimate exchange between speaker and reader, operates as an equalizing technology. No perspective towers over another. No point of reference is too distant to be met with an intimacy and familiarity of regard. A poem's speaker and its reader occupy a uniform plane; both are equal, and equally necessary, in the scheme of the poem. This is true even in a poem like "We Are Not Responsible," where the intimate proximity of reader to speaker fosters neither trust nor a relaxing of defenses. The poem, in mimicking patterns operating in life, insists that the reader scrutinize the hierarchy privileging "We" to the detriment of "You." All sit level as if at the feet of this, the poem's conundrum, which grows large, near, and increasingly familiar in response to our participation in the poem's unfolding. "We" becomes everybody's problem, and all become better versed in the fallacies and failures of logic propping the problem up.

Now, will a poem feed and house you? Will it protect you from the gears of a relentless bureaucracy? No. But it may fortify you in such a way as to better recognize when what you are being offered is "pure wind." And it may instill in you an interest in strangers and an investment in their thoughts and experiences that, in turn, makes you increasingly at ease and at home in a world comprised of all manner of others. Like Dickinson's Nobodyness, poetry is at heart a search and recovery mission ("Then there's a pair of us!"), which rejects the calculated deflections of power-based hierarchies in favor of an active and improvisatory empathy. As with the ultra-black fish in Bulley's erasure, a poem impels its reader to "find / & enter into relations with [an] other" by way of the poem's speaker. In this way, a poem is like an eagerly awaited letter from a stranger.

On Sunday, March 19, 1865, a freedman named George Washington dictates a letter to President Abraham Lincoln. Washington resides on Hilton Head Island in South Carolina, a community liberated from the Confederacy by Union soldiers at the Battle of Port Royal in 1861. Deemed "contrabands," Blacks fleeing enslavement on this island's plantations, as well as those, like Washington, making haste from enslavement on the mainland, have flocked to contraband camps throughout the liberated areas of the South where freedmen, women, and children are housed, given employment, and offered education in dedicated schools. Freedmen aged eighteen to forty-five are also enlisting en masse in the US Army colored regiments. As refugees of a ruthlessly enforced system of Nobodyness—in which they've been denied personhood, held as property, brutalized, bred, and used without recourse to the regard or protection afforded white citizens—Blacks are keenly invested in national politics and the prospect of slavery's official abolition. Washington, who is past the age for military service, has been following Lincoln's political career with tremendous hope at least since the 1860 election. In his letter, he says,

I love you freely. I am now 53 years old. Inauguration day was also my birth-day. I have come 278 miles from Savannah and from there to Hilton Head. I have lain awake four nights and my mind so bore upon you that I could not rest till I sent you a letter. I lived in Butts Co. Ga. I am obliged to send you this to satisfy my mind I wish you all the blessings that can be restored by the Almighty.

Like a poem, sometimes a letter can act, for its author, as a proxy for the ideal recipient, the perfect receptive ear and heart. I can hear in Washington's prose a yearning that goes beyond the desire to connect to Lincoln as a public figure. It is as if Washington is longing not just to make the acquaintance of but rather to *reunite with* a figure who has for some time filled his conscious imagination. I hear an urgency—something like a commitment to repaying a debt—in the statement, "I have lain awake four nights and my mind so bore upon you that I could not rest till I sent you a letter." Lincoln has become one of Washington's intimates, someone alive in his feelings and thoughts—so much so that the author is reduced to a state of unrest that can only be quelled by bringing his feelings into language, and moreover offering them to the person who has inspired them. As if to have inspired someone is to be owed, or even in need of, that person's outpouring of reciprocal thought and emotion.

Were a meeting between the two men imaginable, the spell the letter casts would surely be ruptured by the demands of propriety, by the terms of hierarchy, and by the actual reality of Lincoln as he existed in the world beyond Washington's mind. I imagine such an event, if captured in portrait form, would feature Lincoln beatified in the painting's center foreground, and Washington hugging the margin, shrouded in shadow—like images of Washington's namesake, President George Washington, with William "Billy" Lee, one of the men enslaved to him at Mount Vernon. But this letter, sent less than a month before Lincoln's assassination, becomes a possibility all its own, one in which Washington, who allows himself to expect much of Lincoln in his role of president, is also permitted to repay what he regards as a duty to his private version of Lincoln the man ("I could not rest till I sent you a letter").

Washington continues:

> I would be glad to go back to see my family. I do love my wife and children. I have been a Baptist member for 25 years and I have been praying for this for 17 years. At that time I had a vision and you was made known to me in a dream. I saw a comet come from the North to the South and I said good Lord what is that? I heard a voice "There shall be wars & rumors of wars" I saw many signs and wonders. My soul is filled with joy at the pleasure of letting you know. I have had a heap of high mountains and deep waters to cross. My master threatened my life if I should talk about this. But I just put all my trust in the Lord and I believe he has brought me conqueror through. I give my mind to pray for you the balance of my days.

An essential yet under-tended feature of our shared stewardship of common reality is the ability to see across distances of social status and beyond received notions of worth and due. Maybe it is easy for Washington, mere sentences after professing his love and longing for members of his blood family, to peer up the social ladder toward the President of the United States, whose conscience and political acumen will help to determine whether all Blacks suffering under bondage will be truly and permanently emancipated. Even from the conditions of enslavement, ordinary Blacks like Washington and his family *do* pitch their thoughts and intentions beyond the rungs of the familiar. Given what the familiar holds ("My master threatened my life if I should talk about this . . ."), it is critical that they lift their gaze beyond the known toward the needful, the hopeful, even the nigh impossible. Isn't this in and of itself a likely reason why the letter's author has been named after the nation's first president? Because someone understood that important people and events were indeed relevant to a child born enslaved? I also locate a prodigious power in Washington's visionary imagination, one biblical for sure, with its echoes of the Gospel of Matthew and the book of Acts,[*] but an imagination that is also, in its ability to claim the miraculous as imminent, quite *poetic*. I'm not deploying that word in its generic sense to imply that Washington's letter is simply colorful or expressive. I am talking about poetry as a philosophy of being, which makes Washington willing to leap into a view of reality that admits the essential role of metaphor. This is not to say that Washington does not anticipate the *actual* unfolding of a miraculous turn of events; clearly he has been hoping, then praying, and now dreaming and professing that such a wish might become reality. But he has only been able to commit to such a vision in the first place because of a willingness to pitch his imagining beyond the radius of ordinary occurrence. To start down a path of visioning that begins with

---

[*] Matthew 24:6 reads: "And ye shall hear of wars and rumors of wars: see that ye be not troubled: for all these things must come to pass, but the end is not yet." Acts 2:19 reads: "And I will shew wonders in heaven above, and signs in the earth beneath; blood, and fire, and vapor of smoke."

the declaration, *I want to be free.* And to proceed further still along that route to, *I believe that freedom is a possibility.* And beyond that to assert, *I claim freedom for myself and my loved ones.* And to back that up with, *I accept that freedom is a reality for which my people and I are destined.* Yet Washington takes this trajectory still one step further. In insisting that Lincoln is someone who must be *made to see* ("I had a vision . . .") that his own individual destiny and that of the entire nation are intertwined with Washington's destiny and with the destiny of Washington's entire race, the letter's author posits himself as a messenger—and also an architect—of a radically distinct version of common reality, one in which, to quote from poet Gwendolyn Brooks's poem "Paul Robeson":

> we are each other's
> harvest:
> we are each other's
> business:
> we are each other's
> magnitude and bond.

Washington has awakened from a dream's vision determined to summon Lincoln into the dream of a different waking reality. And while he is not a poet, his letter carries with it the utmost hope of a poem, which is to foster for its reader the freedom to envision another way of being in the world—or another world in which to be.

Like a letter, sometimes a poem can represent, for its reader, an opportunity to embody the ideal recipient, the perfect attentive ear and heart. I'm thinking of a reader capable of meeting the poem not simply with interest or curiosity, nor merely with intelligence and judgment. One who dwells upon a poem only in order to deliver his opinion is reading from a long-occupied position in a common reality still striated into tiers and territories. No, I am describing—and also, like Washington, eagerly hoping to activate—readers willing to open their full feeling selves to being startled, challenged, and even possibly changed by a voice on a page. But how, how do you become such a reader? A glimpse of this state of receptivity may come through when we turn our attention to another urgent letter.

ON NOVEMBER 21, 1864, five months before Washington dictates his letter to Lincoln, Mrs. Jane Welcom,* a widow from Carlisle, Pennsylvania, addresses her own letter to the president:

> Mr abarham lincon   I wont to knw sir if you please wether I can have my son relest from the arme   he is all the subport I have now   his father is Dead and his brother that wase all the help that I had   he has bean wonded twise   he has not had nothing to send me yet   now I am old and my head is blossaming for the grave and if you dou I hope the lord will bless you and me   if you please answer as soon as you can if you please   tha say that you will simpethise with the poor   thear was awhite jentel man told me to write to you   Mrs jane Welcom if you please to answer to it
>
> he be long to the eight regmat co a u st colard troops mart welcome is his name   he is a sarjent

---

* Note that the surname Welcom has been cataloged as "Welcome" across archives, though in this instance I prefer to respect the name as given by the letter's author.

I encountered Mrs. Welcom's petition to have her son released from service while conducting research for a poem commissioned for the National Portrait Gallery's commemoration of the 150th anniversary of the beginning of the Civil War, a war it has always discomfited me to debate. So much of my schooling has emphasized the lingering contention around the "real" cause of the Civil War. States' rights. Northern hostility toward the booming Southern economy. The North's desire to preserve the Union. The one about Confederate soldiers fighting not to defend slavery, but in defense of *the Southern way of life*. In my mind, each of those roads leads back to the Rosetta Stone of slavery. And so, not wanting to add my voice to the chorus of division on what seemed a solemn or even a sacred occasion, I sought to learn as much as I could from the voices of Blacks who had served in the Civil War. Why had they enlisted? What did they believe themselves to be fighting for? And what had their family members hoped for as they awaited news from afar? I suppose I had imagined that studying the testimonies of Black soldiers and their family members would allow me to process their experiences of war in such a way as to attest in my own voice to their sense of what was at stake. Often, in discussing my preliminary understanding of what I was setting out to do in undertaking such a poem, I have used words like *digest* or *metabolize*. As if the research for such a poem was something I had initially understood as a matter of consuming other people's stories, their logics, their very voices and pleas. But it was Mrs. Welcom's letter that disabused me of that notion because of the way—right at the center, right where I imagine its heart to be—it brims with the undeniably affecting poetry of the line "now I am old and my head is blossaming for the grave . . ."

I thought of a pumpkin flower, which takes some time to form on a plant grown from a seed. First is the waiting. The season of new stalks, green leaves stretching out to catch the sun, to be spattered with rain and chewed through by slugs. And then a green-yellow something stretches, and begins to burn more gold than yellow, to unfurl like a new flag under the sun. At its center is a pistil, or ovary. The hope of harvest. What does it mean to blossom *for* the grave? To bear fruit not on the way to death, but for death's very sake? I suppose she is talking about generation—how the generations of a family flow from one another, and how a mother flowers, feeds, and foretells the true fruit—a child. How her work is to ensure that flourishing. To do so, to have done so, is to have completed a vitally important task, not just in one life but in the life of humankind. Mrs. Welcom wants the president to know that she has done just that, and, having kept her two sons sound and alive through so many of life's perilous battles, she has now gone on to watch them offer themselves up to the service of humanity. And what is humanity if not the past, present, and future of common reality? Would the president see fit to grant her son Mart a reprieve to attend to his mother as she wanes and shrinks, as all life must on its way back to dirt?

I was no longer a poet conducting research, but a rapt reader startled and awakened to new registers of urgency and feeling—and a newly tempered understanding of the reality all inhabit—by a voice leaning out from the page, and across the distance of a century and a half, to reach an attending reader. I wonder what President Lincoln would have felt upon receipt of Mrs. Welcom's request. Did he read it before it was forwarded to the Bureau of Colored Troops where it would ultimately be denied? Still, it strikes me that Mrs.

Jane Welcom's voice persists, beyond the war, beyond her lifetime and those of her sons, into every present in which it might be heard and held in heart and mind.*

Is it freedom that has driven us so often to war against ourselves? Not freedom, but our conception of it as an altitude to which some are born, and toward which most must struggle, too often for naught? How we squint up at its peak, shrouded in thick mist. We've been taught so well to discern the sight of it, to know who is at home there and who a guest, that we take this gaze, this way of watching, with us everywhere, casting it upon others, peering through it back at ourselves. But what we permit ourselves to *hear* has bearing upon what we are able to see. And a poem is a voice offering to build the world, by means of some crucial fragment, anew. A voice overcoming all manner of distance in order to soothe or astonish, entreat or rebuke. To ponder what has not yet been seen, what has eluded capture. *To alter, fundamentally, the Forms of our—*

---

* Welcom's letter, reproduced with the addition of line breaks and minimal edits, appears as the opening section to my Civil War poem, "I Will Tell You the Truth About This, I Will Tell You All About It." The poem is a multipart suite composed entirely of letters written by Black Civil War soldiers and their family members, and excerpts of deposition statements given by Black veterans and their descendants and widows in an attempt to claim pensions after the war. On a related note, a pension claim was filed on May 17, 1866, by Martin Welcome of Pennsylvania, who served in the US Army's 8th Regiment, US Colored Infantry. A subsequent claim was filed by Welcome's widow, Katherine A. Welcome, on March 8, 1893. These documents are held by the National Archives and Records Administration.

FEATS OF CONSCIOUSNESS
Poetry Is a Redeeming Act

WHERE DO POEMS come from? From struggle. From feeling lost. From needing to better understand or better accept or better believe the terms of life and reality. A poem is what the poet makes of these forms of unrest. Even a poem of love or celebration is a road map to the realization that joy can be perplexing or unsettling in its power, and must therefore be pondered, grappled with, marveled at. Poetry is a technology by which consciousness can be deployed to undertake this esoteric, existential work.

Francisco Márquez's poem "Provincetown" demonstrates this type of process. Of the poem, Márquez has written, "I often feel unsure or unsatisfied with most of what I write, but this poem was one of the few times it felt different, as if some clear, familiar voice had reached its way through." For me, this statement affirms the sense of a poem is an act of reckoning and offers the hope that individual consciousness might not operate alone, but in concert with other forms of awareness and presence.

Provincetown

Fixed at sunset, a wooden blue shack
as if with it a million scenes of shipwrecks,

not black rock or islands of fog rising individual
in a barrenness of salt. It is not that

it was not beautiful, but that I tried to conjure
its momentous light, eternal

that is inside the ordinary, and couldn't. If I look
backwards, the mysteries forming themselves

in darkness, I remember
the heaviness of heat.

A soporific wave lifting from concrete.
There was more a strangeness

in the dark square of water lifting
from a mallard having submerged,

like the sun into water, than there was
to that wooden place. But to think of it

in exile, in its solitude of water,
to see it turn significant

against what could destroy it,
it was then I saw myself becoming it.

The speaker in Márquez's poem is observing a seascape at sunset when he senses something powerful or sublime about "a wooden blue shack." He wants to name it, but it eludes capture: "I tried to conjure / its momentous light, eternal / that is inside the ordinary, and couldn't."

Where does this poem come from? At least initially from a kind of cognitive failure. The left brain can't answer the question, *Why is the experience of this place meaningful?* And so it is consciousness that rises to the occasion and leads the speaker's gaze inward and backward, toward subjective impressions like "mysteries forming themselves / in darkness," and memories of "the heaviness of heat," "a strangeness / in the dark square of water . . ." There's even a "soporific" (that is to say, a hypnotic or sleep-inducing) "wave lifting from concrete." You might zero in on a line like this, seeking to unravel it into linear clarity. *Is this an image of something liquid or vaporous or solid? Is it heat, haze, or something else? Material or immaterial?* Tell yourself *Yes*. The image offers each of these sensations, and the conflict or confluence of them produces a number of possibilities. One outcome of this image is to unsettle the reader into a multiplicity. A conundrum. Let's admit all of these impressions to the experience of the poem and allow each to do its work. This is one reason why a poem can seem to change from one encounter to the next, even for the same reader.

The observations in Márquez's poem lead us from the features of the external world to the dimensions of the speaker's inner life. At which point he ceases trying to make familiar sense of the physical place and gives himself over to what it evokes for him on a subjective, internal level:

> But to think of it
>
> > in exile, in its solitude of water,
> > to see it turn significant
>
> against what could destroy it,

To be "in exile, in . . . solitude[.]" To exist as an island. To be vulnerable to that which "could destroy" you. (I recognize those feelings. Do you?) The speaker's consciousness offers to project the fragile, lonely human self onto the image of this "wooden blue shack" and to gather from that act of transference a sense of strength and possibility. He sees *himself* becoming "significant // against what could destroy" him. He sees his "ordinary" self becoming "momentous" and "eternal." Even amidst struggle and uncertainty, amidst "a million scenes of shipwrecks" (I've had shipwrecks in my life, have you?) and even in the face of inevitable human difficulty, this view of the self seizes on a kind of invincibility. Some poems make their case like an argument, by a series of steps. Márquez's arrival is a soaring leap the poem makes, a surrender to revelation: "it was then I saw myself becoming it."

I think of Emily Dickinson writing in solitude, sending her poems off in letters or else storing them safely in a drawer in her room. Or the families whose fates hung on the outcome of the Civil War pleading their cases, trusting that their voices would reach the correct ears and cause something to happen. Eventually a poem—a voice—intercepts another consciousness, by which it commences again to travel. This encounter occurs each time a poem is read, received, dwelled with, and carried off into the arc of another life. As if every thought, every utterance, on its way into the reality we share, journeys not just through the layers of an individual self, but through a traffic of many lives. It is an unceasing trajectory, reaching not just those who read the poem, but also the far-flung others imperceptibly touched by the effects of the poem in those who have read it. Such a journey is not unique to poetry. All acts and utterances travel forward and leave behind a wake. Even if unobserved or unremarked, no ripple persists unfelt.

To read or receive a poem, to consent to feel and ponder, to react and even sometimes to reply, all of those are acts with outcomes, even if we seldom seek to measure them. I believe they are redeeming acts in a culture marred by division and diminishment, by rapacious consumption and accelerating scarcity. I would also go so far as to say that the largeness of mind and spirit that poems afford us actually invites our dissatisfaction with the view of the world as a place made up mostly of resources to exhaust or consume, and of other people to judge, mistrust, or instrumentalize. A poem's feats of consciousness—to hear, to see, to feel, to wonder, to doubt, to want, to recognize, to hope, to ache, to redirect, to admit—these and other acts put something vital and irreplaceable into universal circulation.

BE YE NOT AFRAID

A Brief Guide to What Poems Are and How They Do What They Do

———

1. WHAT IS A POEM?

Poems operate from the understanding that the usual behavior of language in which we tend to conduct our everyday business is not enough, not by a long shot, to foster the close, fresh attention that invites true recognition, let alone revelation. Everyday language is too automatic, too entrenched in habit, too deft at dodging candor, let alone vulnerability:

>*How are you?*

>*Fine. You?*

>*Okay. What's new?*

>*Not much. You?*

>*Me, too. Same old same old.*

But doesn't life sometimes make you want to laugh, cry, whisper, and yell? Haven't you ever wished you could pull someone in close so as to see them better or insist they take more careful stock of you? And sometimes, is it not a person you wish to examine or command in such a way, but a circumstance, like death or heartache or fright? In every life, aren't there questions, upsets, and delights it is neither sufficient to feel once and let go, nor to live through and process on your own? We don't just want to *tell* our stories, after all, we want reassurance that they matter and make sense. We want help living as and with ourselves.

On its most basic level, a poem is an invitation to a form of encounter. Someone has sought out the comfort and the company of another for the purpose of disclosing, and thereby making more real and consequential, a vital fragment of their own story. Of course, the first reader of every poem is the poet writing it, a person seeking to engage his, her, or their own most attentive and courageous self in an act of observation and inquiry. The first reader of every poem, the poet writing it, is someone willing to ask questions like *Who am I really? How did I get into this situation? What does it feel like to love, grieve, and fear as me?* The poet calls upon as many versions of self as might be helpful—former and present, individual and member of the collective, courageous soul and knower of fear—in order to more fully grapple with any number of life's questions. So how does a poem bridge the distance between one life and another, or between disparate-seeming facets of a single life? Moreover, how does a poem manage to lead a person—its poet, its reader—from what they may know, or think they know, to what they may have no idea they seek to discover? How do poems and the people who write them go about moving past surface awareness to touch ground in some glimmer of discovery, or even revelation?

Think of the difference between phrases like *Keep calm and carry on** and *Be ye not afraid*.† Both mean nearly the same thing but each lands differently, and the distinction between them is not owing solely to their variations in syntax, compression, or even their authors' aesthetic sensibility. *Keep calm and carry on* encourages the reader to hustle along and get things done; it's designed not to draw a person in nor to invite their questions, but rather to neutralize all notions of struggle and, in their place, encourage stoic compliance. On the other hand, *Be ye not afraid* seeks to halt someone in their tracks, offering to assuage fear in the face of that which is nevertheless large. It is an invitation out toward some aspect of the complex and conflicted world, and also in toward some facet of the complex and conflicted self. These are the directions in which poems encourage us to turn: out beyond the self, and further inward than we are in the everyday habit of going. There are as many different ways to do this as there are poems written, or yet to be. Every poem is an invitation to its reader and writer alike to pay closer, fuller, and more courageous attention.

---

* Text of a British Ministry of Information poster drafted to boost morale during WWII. Though it failed to be brought into circulation as a wartime slogan, the phrase was popularized in 2000 when a copy of the poster surfaced.
† A version of this phrase is spoken various times in the King James Bible by angels and prophets channeling the voice of God.

2. WHO IS SPEAKING?

In her poem "The Crystal Gazer," Sara Teasdale explores the determination to restore oneself to fullness and composure. In the poem, this feat is likened to an act of sorcery:

> *The Crystal Gazer*
>
> I shall gather myself into myself again,
>   I shall take my scattered selves and make them one,
> Fusing them into a polished crystal ball
>   Where I can see the moon and the flashing sun.
>
> I shall sit like a sibyl, hour after hour intent,
>   Watching the future come and the present go,
> And the little shifting pictures of people rushing
>   In restless self-importance to and fro.

This poem, published in 1926, doesn't much deviate from the usual diction and syntax of colloquial American speech, but its logical process is deliberate in elaborating the terms of a personal resolution, and illuminating the sense of difficulty characterizing the speaker's present circumstance. She has come apart. Broken into many pieces. But it wasn't always this way. Her "scattered selves" were once unified and whole. That's what the word "again" signals to me at the end of the first line. That something has agitated her out of her natural and original state.

The term *scatterbrain* has been in circulation in the English language since at least the late eighteenth century, referring to someone whose thoughts are careless and disjointed, in many places at once. In more recent usage, *scatterbrain* and "scattered" belong to a class of words (among them *ditsy, flighty, hysterical,* and *shrill*) that tend to operate as gendered dismissals. The poem's evocation of this familiar figure of speech makes the implicitly female state of being "scattered" into something as concrete and literal as broken glass, at which point the poem seizes on the possibility of "[f]using" the shards back together. Not only is this act of repair pleasing—it will turn "them into a polished crystal ball"—it also promises to restore power and focus to the embattled speaker.

What has ruptured her focus? The poem withholds the details of her larger narrative, but the power she seeks reveals something of what has been withheld from her in her current circumstance. She wants to "see the moon and the flashing sun" and to "sit . . . hour after hour intent, / Watching the future come and the present go[.]" In other words, she yearns to determine the terms of her own relationship to time. The reclamation of time is such a vital feature of the poem that the very first thing the speaker does is to step out of the present verb tense and into the future. And not just any future tense. Recurring three times across the poem's brief span of eight lines, "I shall" infuses the poem with insistence, and with something resembling the formality of a binding legal contract. For the poem's speaker, "I shall" is a means of bucking the addled and put-upon present in order to take charge of herself in, and across, time.

Does the speaker of "The Crystal Gazer" correlate to the poet? Perhaps. But the voice in this or any poem might just as easily belong to someone who is not the poet at all—some other real or imagined persona through whom the poet has elected to speak. Why? Because we are larger than we appear to be, aren't we, you and I? We spill at times beyond the borders we're taught to abide—past expectations of family, gender, class, past all manner of enforced allegiances—to care and wish and wonder more than we've been told we're entitled to. Part of the power of reading poetry is the probability that some facet of the speaker's processing of their own experience will spill into you, the reader, striking you as relevant and even somehow familiar to your own life or mindset. In this particular poem, that kind of recognition occurs swiftly for me. By the end of the second line's "I shall take my scattered selves and make them one," the voice in my own head is sighing in identification and saying, *Me, too!* And so I'm inclined to believe that all poems, even those most faithfully grounded in a poet's actual biography, invite both poet and reader to swell beyond the limits of their own fixed identities, and to test forms of courage and authority, or even simply degrees of rhetorical drama, that everyday life, for whatever reason, holds out of reach. This is one reason for the literary convention of referring to the voice operating within a poem not as a narrator (too fixed and remote) nor as the poet (too binding) but as the poem's *speaker*, a figure with permission to draw upon various sources of actual or longed-for power.

The sibyls were female seers or oracles prophesying the future throughout the ancient world. Unlike witches, hags, or crones, the power of the sibyl is not undermined by connotations of ill temper, decrepitude, or malevolence. Taking recourse to the emphatic and positive female power of the sibyl, Teasdale's speaker rises easily above the usual ceiling of possibility typically afforded any woman, or any human, to adopt a gaze of cool objectivity onto the human plane. From this degree of remove, she's able to recognize the terms of pressure, worth, haste, and duty with which we humans have been saddled. As small as all are revealed to be, in this larger scheme, the speaker witnesses the further diminishment we bring upon ourselves. No longer distinct, the sight of humanity is that of "little shifting pictures of people rushing / In restless self-importance to and fro."

It's an alarming image. But I'd argue it's more bearable to scrutinize the vulnerable self at this double remove: through the eyes of a seer, and en masse in the throng of humankind. The poem becomes a mental exercise in asking, there alongside its first-person speaker, *Whose world is this? What chases us? Must we—and shall I—continue to run?*

3. THE TITLE

A poem's title, there at the top of the page, is an occasion for anticipation, and a source of questions and expectations that the poem will soon enough confirm or deflect, answer or redirect. No title is accidental. Even a poem without a title, or one employing "Untitled" in that space, is intending and announcing something. And though it's exciting to descend into the world of the poem, it's worth hovering at that level for a moment, like an aircraft in a holding pattern, above the poem's first line. How are you being prepared for descent into the territory of the poem?

What are you led to wonder, gather, or anticipate as a result of the title of this next poem, by Edna St. Vincent Millay? And how do the stages of entry into the body of the poem serve to validate or temper those initial questions and expectations?

Assault

I.

I had forgotten how the frogs must sound
After a year of silence, else I think
I should not have so ventured forth alone
At dusk upon this unfrequented road.

II.

I am waylaid by Beauty. Who will walk
Between me and the crying of the frogs?
Oh, savage Beauty, suffer me to pass,
That am a timid woman, on her way
From one house to another!

At the sight of the title "Assault," I'm made to feel protective of someone, and also fearful that I myself will need strength or courage to properly attend to their story. I suppose I am also bracing myself for the moment when an attack of some kind might be narrated. These feelings might be even stronger for a reader whose personal experience of assault is activated by the title. What I would like to say about that is: Your memory equips you to hold and extend empathy for and to others, even the real or imagined speaker of a poem like this one, published more than a century ago in 1921. Empathy of this kind is a vital capacity to acknowledge and honor. It might even allow your own past pain to be a resource rather than a barrier to your encounter of this or any poem. I've found that an emotional hurdle of this kind can be managed by acknowledging something like, *I have been hurt, and my own pain returns to me now as I move toward the speaker of this poem, who may also be vulnerable.* Or, *I am afraid, and my fear accompanies me as I prepare to listen to what the speaker of this poem has to say.* Remember that poetry is not solely a *feeling* art form, but one in which the immediacy of a sometimes-powerful feeling is tempered by the discernment of reason and the agility and resourcefulness of associative thinking. Importantly, as readers drawing upon a concert of faculties, we can be useful witnesses to the presence of grief, sorrow, pain, and fear in the world, and agents of stabilizing clarity, compassion, and courage. Fight-or-flight responses that threaten to disrupt us in the midst of lived fright can thus be offset by the presence of these other steadying capacities.

Passing my gaze over the body of the poem, I see that it has been divided into two sections. I wonder how they will operate in relation to one another, and if the something that will illuminate the poem's title might be located in one or the other of the poem's sections.

The first sense to be mentioned in the poem is that of sound, though not in a way that describes or classifies what is heard: "I had forgotten how the frogs must sound / After a year of silence." If a reader is made to hear anything, it is but noise or the absence of noise. Other key images have to do with time ("a year" and "dusk") and degrees of isolation ("alone," and "unfrequented road"). More than bringing me into a vividly configured place, I'm brought to wonder what has happened? Why does the speaker seem to be emerging from a year of silence? And why such solitude? Did she go away and come back? Has she isolated herself by choice?

So far, the only assault to occur in the poem is one of sensory impact, though the final two lines of this section clearly emerge from the mind of a person cognizant of her own vulnerability: "I think / I should not have so ventured forth alone / At dusk upon this unfrequented road." I register the awareness of danger in these phrases, and shades of the customary warning that trouble tends to crop up in desolate, "unfrequented" locations. The possibility of threat inhabits the poem, not solely in the physical features of its setting ("dusk" and "road"), but also, and perhaps more so, in the memory and imagination of its speaker.

Like the poem's speaker, we readers are traveling. We pass through the break between the first and second sections, which feels itself like an "unfrequented road," to find white space: silence which may not necessarily be absence, but rather a form of anticipation. And when we reach section two, the speaker takes on a wider view of her own situation. She classifies it: "I am waylaid by Beauty." She also shifts, slightly, the nature of her address. No longer is she strictly speaking to herself or even to her reader; with the arrival of the line, "Oh, Savage Beauty, suffer me to pass," she lifts her awareness beyond the human to address her plea to the invisible forces within the landscape. She's startled into this new awareness not by the shock or threat of harm, which she has been conditioned to expect, but rather the beauty of the natural world, a setting widely believed to soothe, restore, and comfort the otherwise afflicted. Nevertheless, the speaker pleads, "suffer me to pass," as if the terms of consolation and affront have been inverted.

If section two ultimately infuses the poem with relief—all remains safe and well in the poem—it also makes use of words that authorize and sustain a reader's reasons for being on alert. The presence of the word "suffer," which means *allow* in this context, also subtly plants in the poem its more typical conventional connotation of *pain* or *torment*. "Who will walk / Between" emphasizes the speaker's wish for a guardian or escort to shield and protect her. Though the word "crying" refers to the singing of the frogs, its presence also makes the poem into a context where it would be unsurprising to find tears. And while I find evidence to support the view that the poem's speaker is large and feeling, passionate and brave in her living, the self-portrait of "a timid woman, on her way / From one house to another" does not eradicate cause for worry. To come away from this poem feeling merely relief at the absence of violence might amount to a willful avoidance of the much that the poem's speaker has been made, for reasons that remain outside of the poem, to fear. In other words, though there is no active threat in her immediate vicinity, she is nevertheless vulnerable by dint of who she is and what previous experience has taught her. This circumstance becomes, for me, the mortar between the poem's two sections. Awareness of our own vulnerability accompanies many of us even into contexts where the only startlement is that which arises in response to the surprise of our own welcome and safety.

Now, having read through and considered the entire poem, try going back up to the title and repeating the descent. Upon a second or even a third reading, what are you led to recognize or discover about the work done by the poem's title?

4. IMAGES

Images flood the body with sensory information, drawing a poem's reader—and also its poet—into a feeling of credible proximity to and even participation in the events and feelings the poem explores. Images are therefore essential to poetry. Without them, poet and reader are constrained to imagine or recollect from a distance, and from a place of thought or abstraction rather than one of visceral engagement.

Images aren't only about making a poem vivid and realistic feeling—though they certainly do these things. Importantly for the poet, they also create a visceral pathway into the poem's material. If you can get your senses there—if you can make a sensory connection, even via memory or imagination, to a place you know or once knew, or even to one you are inventing on the spot—some sliver of your consciousness can travel there and report back. Try it: Go back in memory to the room where you slept as a child. Stretch out on the bed or the floor. Touch and peer closely at the walls. Handle objects. Breathe in the smells of that place and time. What further feelings and impressions begin to return to you now? If you persist in this fashion, it's quite likely that emotional insights will begin to ride in on the heels of these sensory memories.

John Yau's "Music from Childhood" is an immersive lyric in which an adult speaker seems to address his child-self via the second-person pronoun "you." Things heard, seen, dreamt, and remembered occur and recur throughout the poem, which adheres to the pattern of repetition associated with the *pantoum* form, in which every individual line repeats once later in the poem:

Music from Childhood

You grow up hearing two languages. Neither fits your fits
Your mother informs you "moon" means "window to another world"

You begin to hear words mourn the sounds buried inside their mouths
A row of yellow windows and a painting of them

Your mother informs you "moon" means "window to another world"
You decide it is better to step back and sit in the shadows

A row of yellow windows and a painting of them
Someone said you can see a blue pagoda or a red rocket ship

You decide it is better to step back and sit in the shadows
Is it because you saw a black asteroid fly past your window

Someone said you can see a blue pagoda or a red rocket ship
I tried to follow in your footsteps, but they turned to water

Is it because I saw a black asteroid fly past my window
The air hums—a circus performer riding a bicycle towards the ceiling

I tried to follow in your footsteps, but they turned to water
The town has started sinking back into its commercial

> The air hums—a circus performer riding a bicycle towards
>   the ceiling
> You grow up hearing two languages. Neither fits your fits
>
> The town has started sinking back into its commercial
> You begin to hear words mourn the sounds buried inside
>   their mouths*

Nearly all sense or logic in the poem is filtered through close-range, subjective impressions rather than linear narrative. As a result, the speaker's investment in journeying back or calling out toward the terms of his own childhood lines up with the reader's experience of getting acquainted with the features of another person's memory. This dynamic is succinctly established in the poem's opening *couplet*, or two-line stanza: "You grow up hearing two languages. Neither fits your fits / Your mother informs you 'moon' means 'window to another world[.]'"

We learn that the poem's speaker was raised in a dual-language household, or perhaps that, as with many families, there was an intimate language that differed in some way from the language with which the outside world was navigated. This is the first of several dualities the stanza introduces. Another is the dual sense of the word "fits," which we may take to mean the ability of one thing to contain or accommodate another, and also an outburst resulting when emotions rupture the bounds of an expected norm. In line two, the word "moon" erupts into a second meaning. In what way is the moon

---

* The long lines in couplets 1, 2, 3, 7, 9, and 10 in Yau's poem have been broken to accommodate this book's page size. Indented lines reflect line breaks that do not appear in the original poem.

a window? What and where is the other world that it frames? How many worlds can there be, and might a person manage to feel at home in any of them? Pondering these shifting terms, which are visual in some ways and philosophical in others, serves to draw us nearer to the feelings and forms of imagination brimming in the speaker's childhood.

Sound-based images—specifically, instances of voices heard or overheard—also play an important role in the poem, making up a part of the "music" in the poem's title. Take for instance the line "Someone said you can see a blue pagoda or a red rocket ship[.]" Whose words were those? To what were they referring? Was it a painting, a picture book, or something more actual? Again, it is questions that draw readers into a process of seeking or gathering, which is analogous to memory's task of recollecting. Listening also helps a reader to process an image like "You begin to hear words mourn the sounds buried inside their mouths." What sounds? The sound of things regretted or left unsaid? The sound of one language supplanting another? Sonically, the words "mourn," "sounds," "buried," and "mouths" work together to create a heavy tone, owing perhaps to their vowels' association with the actual sound of moaning or howling. I think of people growing apart from one another. I think of loss or disappointment. The insular space of a family with its generational forgetting and remembering is one obvious context for these impressions, but patterns of change, erasure, and grief also operate at the scale of the individual; they are functions of memory itself.

The poem's progression through these fragmentary, uncontextualized memories is swift and unencumbered by transitions. It is line breaks, rather than periods, that do the work of separating discrete statements from one another. Each new line snaps us into a new scene, a new form of awareness. In this manner, the poem averts or subverts the expectation of narrative continuity, emphasizing instead the unit of the line as the poem's dominant frame. As a line ends, so ends a memory or a vignette, even sometimes mid-statement.

If a poem's setting is the container for its narrative (or lyric) unfolding, and its formal structure (which we'll touch upon in the next section) comprises the architecture through which the reader is guided, then its images work to exert a sense of psychic or emotional atmosphere. In another poem, that atmosphere might be fixed or stable, but in "Music from Childhood," emotions dawn and crest, wane and set. The hope of a line like "I tried to follow in your footsteps" is transformed into abandonment upon the arrival of "but they turned to water[.]" The self-negation of "You decide it is better to step back and sit in the shadows" is intercepted by the startlement of seeing "a black asteroid fly past your window[.]"

Does childhood end? Yes. And no. Yau's poem reminds us that it surfaces again and again in a life, familiar and strange, through the fragments and figments of memory.

5. FORM

"Music from Childhood" modifies the stanzaic pattern of the traditional pantoum. This innovation upon an existing form feels important. When a poet like Yau uses—while also pushing against—the conventions of a traditional or received form, he's making a statement. He's saying to the formal tradition, *You have something I need, and I have something to offer you*. In this fashion, the form is adapted to new use. I'm of the opinion that received forms—sonnets, ghazals, villanelles, pantoums, and so forth—are perennial precisely because they're nimble enough to be at home in so many subjects, so many different aesthetic sensibilities and contexts. As durable architecture, these forms can accommodate renovation while also remaining recognizable as themselves. The inverse also bears stating: For the effects of innovation to be felt, and felt as worthwhile, the form must also remain recognizable as itself. So let's talk briefly about the traditional behavior of the pantoum.

In a strict or traditional pantoum, the second and fourth lines of one four-line stanza, or *quatrain*, become the first and third lines of the subsequent quatrain. The pattern comes full circle in the poem's final stanza, whose second and fourth lines make use of what were originally the first and third lines to appear in the poem's opening stanza. That's it. A pantoum can be any length, and it can employ a rhyme-scheme or metrical pattern if the poet so chooses, but it needn't. Many practitioners of the form make minor variations in some but not all of the repeated lines. Such variations might include changes in punctuation or word form that introduce the feeling not solely of recurrence but also of subtle development. Again, this isn't a fixed feature of the form, but something that can be seen to add surprise and individuality to a poet's engagement with received form— but as with innovation in general, for the effects of minor variations to be felt, and felt as worthwhile, the pantoum's repeated lines must also retain resemblance to one another.

Intrinsic to the pantoum form is the improbability that its pattern of repetition is something a reader comes to readily anticipate; lines would have to repeat more than once for that to be the case. Instead a pantoum, especially on a first reading, creates an eerie sense of déjà vu, the feeling of having foreseen something without quite understanding how. It's a useful pattern for considering the field of memory, with all its hauntings and aberrations.

The quatrain, as a stanzaic form, has long been adept at sustaining the weight of narrative without becoming overladen or bogged down. Quatrains also adapt readily to the effects of meter and rhyme, which aids in their memorization. That's why ballads, prayers, hymns, and pop lyrics often take the form of rhymed quatrains.

As an aside, every stanzaic pattern demonstrates character traits that inform how a reader perceives and moves through the field of a poem, but none are set in stone; poets can make choices that amplify or temper these intrinsic traits. One-line stanzas feel emphatic, aphoristic, even spotlit; a poem written entirely of one-line stanzas might bear some resemblance to a bulleted list or a manifesto. Couplets naturally lend themselves to exploring the degrees of tension between pairs of things seeking to operate as a single unit. Like a graceful juggling act, three-line stanzas, or *tercets*, somersault forward while also allowing each line to rise to the reader's attention. The names of other common stanza lengths are *quintets*, or five-line stanzas; *sextets*, or six-line stanzas; *septets*, or seven-line stanzas; *octaves*, or eight-line stanzas; *nonets*, or nine-line stanzas. Ten-line stanzas are called *décimas*, but you'll notice that beyond a certain point, the effects of stanza length frankly become less perceptible than the shifts or redirections characterizing the breaks between stanzas.

When Yau's "Music from Childhood" swaps out the quatrains normally associated with the pantoum for couplets, the quatrain's facility with managing the cause and effect of narrative is ceded to the couplet's adeptness exploring the tensions within dualities. Additionally, the white space between couplets stretches out the visual field of the poem just enough to make the pantoum's pattern of repetition harder to see, thereby delaying the moment when a reader might realize, *Aha! I know where I am! I've been here before!* Maybe that's part of the point. The reader's surprise at sudden recognition is relevant to the speaker's investment in unearthing his own buried memories.

If Yau's were the only pantoum you'd ever read, you might come away with the impression of the form as gestural and fragmentary, but it can be quite narrative, as well. As a point of comparison, let's observe Natasha Trethewey's use of the form in her poem "Incident," which, like "Music from Childhood," also happens to be a twenty-line pantoum written in reflection of events occurring during the speaker's childhood. As the poem states in its opening line, the telling and retelling of this particular memory is a form of ritual, something the pantoum's built-in repetitions serve to emphasize and replicate.

Incident

We tell the story every year—
how we peered from the windows, shades drawn—
though nothing really happened,
the charred grass now green again.

We peered from the windows, shades drawn,
at the cross trussed like a Christmas tree,
the charred grass still green. Then
we darkened our rooms, lit the hurricane lamps.

At the cross trussed like a Christmas tree,
A few men gathered, white as angels in their gowns.

> We darkened our rooms and lit hurricane lamps,
> The wicks trembling in their fonts of oil.
>
> It seemed the angels had gathered, white men in their gowns.
> When they were done, they left quietly. No one came.
> The wicks trembled all night in their fonts of oil;
> by morning the flames had all dimmed.
>
> When they were done, the men left quietly. No one came.
> Nothing really happened.
> By morning all the flames had dimmed.
> We tell the story every year.

In contrast to Yau's couplets, which heighten the reader's experience of discrete and potentially discontinuous slivers and fragments of memory, Trethewey's quatrains lead from beginning, to middle, to the seeming end of a remembered encounter with members of the Ku Klux Klan, a narrative that operates by way of the pronoun "we." Just as the first-person plural anchors the poem's speaker within her family, I'd argue that the pronoun "we" also gathers the reader into the position of intimate witness to the poem's events. If you are curious as to how this pronoun choice serves to heighten a reader's involvement in the poem and its events, go back and read the poem aloud.

Though invested in a specific narrative, Trethewey's poem doesn't prioritize a full play-by-play of dramatic action. Instead, it emphasizes the unholy quiet and terrifying inaction surrounding the remembered events. All these years later, what stands out to the poem's speaker about the memory in question—what haunts her still—is how understated so much of it seemed. The perpetrators were free to go about their business with the authority of "the angels[.]" "When they were done, they left quietly. No one came." The poem's only allusion to fear and vulnerability—which, like every other image, appears twice—is offloaded from the family members in the poem, who must have felt pressure to guard their calm in the midst of such fright, onto the lamp wicks, which "trembled all night in their fonts of oil[.]" Owing to its diction, the personification of lamp wicks trembling as if in empathy with human suffering feels biblical. Like a minor miracle. It also emphasizes the dearth of human allies in the scene.

If we look at where the poem begins and where it ends, we'll see examples of how momentum can be accrued across lines in a poem, as well as how deceleration can be enforced. We'll also observe how minor variations in a line from one iteration to the next can create shifts in emphasis and meaning.

Each line in the opening quatrain is end-stopped; its punctuation urges us to pause and parse as the sense of the sentence, which stretches over the full span of the quatrain, accumulates:

> We tell the story every year—
> how we peered from the windows, shades drawn—
> though nothing really happened,
> the charred grass now green again.

The stanza, as it moves toward the full completion of the sentence upon which it rides, also leads us through time: from the *years ago* in which "the story" can be understood to have occurred, and the cyclical recurrence of "every year," through to the terminus of "now" in the stanza's final line. In the middle of the stanza, the qualification, "though nothing really happened," tempers or downplays the poem's central event even before it has occurred. Look: The site upon which it occurred has grassed back in "green again." Or maybe this understatement operates in similar fashion to the way the phrase *Nothing to see here, folks* is used to hustle onlookers away from the scene of an accident or a crime. In other words, maybe it is a subtle acknowledgment that something—indeed, something still sensitive in nature—has taken place. We'll be able to judge the incident for ourselves soon enough.

Now compare the first stanza's qualifications and subterfuges to the final quatrain, in which similar language operates to different dramatic effect:

> When they were done, the men left quietly. No one came.
> Nothing really happened.
> By morning all the flames had dimmed.
> We tell the story every year.

That long, two-sentence line at the top of the final quatrain occupies the same unit of measure—a line—as the three-word sentence below. And so the shorter line commands more emphasis. Why? If the line is a unit of real estate in a poem, each with the same inherent value, then the line packed with three steps of the story, which the reader hurries along its span to gather, puts us in something of a rush. It's got more noise in it, more details, more stages or stations of thought. But the short line can afford to take its time. It says one thing only. And the period following upon the word "happened," trailed by so much more white space than the lines above and below it, equates in a subtle way to something like emphasis. Silence, as visual white space in a poem, is rarely if ever absence. Rather, it is indication of a space so charged with feeling and reverberation that even devoid of text it must be held and felt.

Naturally, even unconsciously, we offer a greater degree of attention to "Nothing really happened." Attention enough to recognize that something has changed since we've seen the phrase before. This time, it foregoes the qualification of "though," which marked its first go-round up in stanza one. And this time, it's airtight and inarguable, owing to the period calling the line/statement/sentence to a close. And look at the difference between "the charred grass now green," which emphasizes things making their way back to normal, and "By morning all the flames had dimmed," which calls up one last glimpse of the conflagration before letting it die down to just a smolder. Something *has* happened here, this deliberate behavior of line, pacing, and imagery insists. Something worth remembering. Something we must promise not to forget.

Trethewey's title asserts her poem's indebtedness to the 1927 poem "Incident" by Harlem Renaissance poet Countee Cullen. Cullen's "Incident" also features an adult speaker recounting the indelible memory of a childhood encounter with racism. Trethewey's title is an acknowledgment of the poetic tradition in which her poem and Cullen's participate—one that has chosen to bear witness to the effects of collective history upon the individual Black psyche. A version of the memory from which Trethewey's "Incident" arises is also narrated in prose form in her 2020 nonfiction work *Memorial Drive: A Daughter's Memoir*, further illustrating the ways that the dialogue from which a poem springs, and to which it contributes, can span forms, time periods, and contexts. Importantly, it reminds us that a single poem, let alone an individual poet, can be consciously operating in more than one tradition at a time. Both Trethewey and Yau draw upon and contribute to the tradition of poems written in contemplation of their authors' heritage. And their poems "Incident" and "Music from Childhood" participate in the tradition of poems written in recollection of childhood. Each also contributes meaningfully to the tradition of the pantoum, extending the reach of the form and expanding its audience. Poets live in a perpetual and ongoing conversation: invoking and responding to their predecessors, inspiring and activating literary offspring, and even circling back to revise and reinvent themselves via alternate forms, new subject matter, and ever-evolving values.

6. A POEM'S CLOSURE

One of the most frequently asked questions I receive as a poet is: *What determines when and how a poem of yours will end?* I think the question itself is a reader's way of acknowledging the powerful effect a poem's ending can have upon a reader. A poem's ending can reiterate something that has come before—in the title, perhaps, or the body of the poem—while also all of a sudden imbuing that word or phrase with new layers of significance. Or it can mark the instant when the speaker is able to recognize or admit something that would have been impossible at the outset of the poem. Out of nowhere, a poem might end on a question without answering it, or an image without elaborating on it. A poem's arrival at its unpremeditated destination will coincide with the dawning of unanticipated discovery or realization. In this, it will feel like the shock of birdsong, or a flash of lightning. Do you hear that: *All of a sudden . . . instant . . .*

out of nowhere . . . unpremeditated . . . unanticipated . . . shock . . . flash? There's something about a poem's ending that eludes anticipation. Even for a reader who can clearly see the blank space ahead in the distance trailing the poem's final line, what it feels like to get there is always, ideally, a kind of miracle—perhaps because whatever else characterizes a poem's closure, it initiates a process meant to continue on for some time outside of the poem, and within the reader.

Anne Spencer's "Dunbar" announces itself as an homage to the poet Paul Laurence Dunbar, who died of tuberculosis in 1906 at the age of thirty-three. Though the two poets never met, Spencer and Dunbar were born within a decade of one another. Both of Dunbar's parents, and Spencer's father, were born into slavery in Kentucky and Virginia, respectively. Spencer, who was raised in Virginia, worked for many years as a librarian at the Washington, DC, high school named in Dunbar's honor.

Dunbar

> Ah, how poets sing and die!
> Make one song and Heaven takes it;
> Have one heart and Beauty breaks it;
> Chatterton, Shelley, Keats and I—
> Ah, how poets sing and die!

This five-line poem, though brief, is rich with implications. For one thing, the title invites the possibility that the speaker of the poem is Dunbar himself, reflecting upon his own life and premature death. And the poem's first line locates something profound in the occasion of having lived not just as a human being, but as a poet. I hear the word *awe* audible in the "Ah" that opens the poem. Be it made manifest as shock, wonderment, or overwhelm, awe is indeed what leads a poet to write—or "sing." Awe is also the aim toward which a poet's voice, via their poems, is pitched. In this sense, one of the first conundrums offered by the poem hovers around the notion that any poem might, on some level, emerge from and return to the same state while also managing, in a perceptible way, to *get somewhere*. Since the poem's first and final lines are identical, this circumstance has particular relevance to the closure, or arrival, of Spencer's poem.

Rhythmically, the poem's prevalent meter is *trochaic tetrameter*, meaning that each line is made up of four metrical units called *trochees*. A trochee is composed of one hard stress followed by one soft stress. (The word *trochee*, pronounced TRO-kee, is itself a trochee.) If you speak the poem's second and third lines aloud (and I hope you will), you'll hear that their natural rhythmic emphasis sounds something like *DUM-dah DUM-da DUM-da DUM-da*.

Prosody is the study of meter in poetry. But for the purpose of discussing the effects of this poem's rhythmic patterns, there is value in simply noting that the poem's movement from hard to soft stresses can be felt to *fall*. (*Rising* meter would move from soft to hard stresses, like a heartbeat: *Da-DUM Da-DUM Da-DUM Da-DUM*.) Spencer attaches her poem's falling meter to the association of death with absence and loss. Indeed, the poem's first and last lines replace the soft stress of the final trochee with silence—as if the exclamation "die!" must necessarily be followed by a hush.

Descending further into the poem, lines two and three operate in consideration of things a poet is made to give away or entrust to the world:

> Make one song and Heaven takes it;
> Have one heart and Beauty breaks it;

What becomes of a poet's work once it is in Heaven's hands? Often, it is not the fate of the poet to decide or even to know the answer to this question. Dunbar, for example, was celebrated in his lifetime for the poems he wrote using African American dialect, which captured what might to him have been the familiar voices of kin born into slavery in Kentucky. Those particular rhythms and vernacular constructions preside in Dunbar's most popular poems, bearing their own complications. Certain of Dunbar's readers, advocating for racial progress and opportunity, resented the ways that the use of dialect threatened to pigeonhole Black life. Yet when Dunbar veered from dialect to write in what we might describe as literary English, his work was often overlooked by critics and publishers who preferred the exoticization of "Negro" speech. It must have seemed to Dunbar that a portion of his poetic "song" went unheard, or languished as misunderstood. Spencer's poem is written in part to attest to the enduring value of Dunbar's legacy.

Reading "Dunbar" as a persona poem, the penultimate line, "Chatterton, Shelley, Keats and I—" stands as the moment when Dunbar introduces a correction to his own harshest critics by enshrining himself alongside seminal figures of the Romantic Movement, young men of genius and conviction who, like Dunbar, died premature deaths. The line holds a powerful charge within the poem, not only because of the achievement attached to these figures, but also because it introduces a perceptible shift in rhythm into the poem. In prosody, the name "Chatterton" is not a trochee but a *dactyl*

(DUM-da-da). It literally sounds like waltzing. The effect of this shift in the poem's music, which we feel even if we lack the technical vocabulary with which to name it, is to render the line into a kind of dance: *Chatterton, Shelley, Keats and I—Chatterton, Shelley, Keats and I—Chatterton, Shelley, Keats and I—* Put differently, the music of the line transmutes the tone operating in the poem, and with it the logic, from one of lament or even rebuke to one of joy. As a result, the word "die" in the poem's closing line—"Ah, how poets sing and die!"—is liberated to operate differently than it did at the outset. Death becomes a unique phenomenon for poets, whose words live on, circulating across time to reach and touch countless lives. Wasn't it Chatterton, Shelley, Keats, and others who helped summon Dunbar to his vocation as a poet? And Dunbar who helped to summon Spencer to hers?

What if the whole of a poet's lifetime—all the many poems and commitments making up a career—are but elements of a single, large, varied, ongoing song? And what if that song is composed of many poets' voices, or of *all* poets' voices? Holding such a possibility in mind, a poet's natural awe (that state ever-audible within the vocalization "Ah") is no longer snatched away; it is admitted into whatever Heaven must be. And the heart—of the poet, of the reader—is no longer bound to be broken, but rather overwhelmed by the world's preponderance of Beauty, and mystery. This is where Spencer's closure leaves me upon this encounter of her poem.

A poem's closure is not a fixed lesson or a message, nor an unchanging view of the poem or the world as a whole, but rather a momentary waystation where, in this single instance, the music and reason of language can be seen to have arrived. Ideally, and perhaps a tad idealistically, a poem's closure marks the beginning of an off-site process of feeling and awareness, which the reader carries away from the page and, for a time, into their own living.

7. ON JUDGMENT

As a reader, I sometimes wonder why there is so much interest in deciding whether a poem is *good* or *bad*, *better* or *worse*, when the relative success of a poem—by which I mean whether and how it hits home—has so much to do with a reader's capacity for attention, and with the degree of associative resourcefulness they bring to the act of reading. A poem might leave one reader cold not because it has failed in its aims, but because that person is, for the time being, uninterested in the stakes of the poem's chosen material. Taste alone as an arbiter of worth is unreliable. Often it bends to the reader's desire to feel comfortable, safe, and in control as opposed to startled or even discomfited beyond the consolations of the known.

More than trying to discern (or to prove) whether or not a poem is *good*, I believe it is worthwhile to identify the specific craft-based choices its poet has made, and the forms of feeling, recognition, awareness, and discovery that follow forth from them. If you are a writer reading to learn, these choices will become tools that might be lifted from another poet's material and carried over into yours, where you may make similar or different use of them. And if you are a reader seeking to understand and describe poems more confidently, these tools will allow you to speak in concrete and specific terms about the ways—and the ends to which—a poem operates.

One of the reasons for my emphasis on observation over judgment is that a poem you don't like on a taste level can still teach you something useful about how a poem can be written and what it might attempt to do. Another extends from the belief that poems do not emerge from the wish to appeal to a reader's taste or judgment, but rather to grapple productively with a question, problem, or conundrum. When I am writing a poem, I'm seeking clarity and fright, the kind of brush with truth the prophet Moses is said to have had before staggering back down from the mountain with stone tablets in hand and hair that had been startled white.

However, when I do consent to think about the degree to which a poem can be understood to succeed (and as an editor and educator, I do find myself in such a position), it's most helpful for me to attempt to do so from the position of a writer looking with rigor and care at the terms of craft operating within a given poem, rather than as a reader wishing to be validated in my discernment. *What has the poem set out to do? What questions does it ask? In what ways does the poem go about elaborating its task? Which possibilities do these choices activate, and which do they shut down?* These questions urge me to read, firstly and mostly, to get to know the poem. *What are its values in language? What words and patterns in sound does it prize? What risks does it take? What aspects of the recognizable world has it rendered anew? What that was at first strange or unfamiliar has it taught me to recognize? What does it render with visceral immediacy, and where does it find, or go looking for, mystery? What forms of pressure or tension complicate or counterbalance the pleasures of beauty in the poem?*

When I'm editing my own early drafts, my questions are blunter: *Where am I bored? Where have I fallen back on my own known tics and habits and what new challenges must I accept in their stead? Where have I held back out of fear? Where have I been showing off out of arrogance?*

The answers to these questions alert me to areas of weakness that must be modulated, abandoned, or reenvisioned. They charge me to go in search of different tools and strategies with which to raise my own writerly stakes. They send me to the school of other poets' work. And to the work of dancers, musicians, and historians. Journalists and mystics. Birds, trees, rocks, rain, dirt.

At times in my teaching, I encounter poems that mistake themselves for essays. They state a thesis and diligently deliver evidence in service of its proof. They determine from the outset where they intend to arrive, and they follow a logical path to get there. In seeking to challenge these writers, I might ask if the poem can instead operate by way of questions. Preferably ones to which they don't, and may never, hold the answers.

Other times, I encounter poems overladen with characters, dialogue, plot, backstories, and fastidiously rendered settings. I might ask such a writer, who has mistaken their poem for a story or a novel, to embrace the compression, repetition, music, and insistence of a strict and concise lyric form like the villanelle.

When a poem mistakes itself for a song, its poet has not yet learned to allow the values of melody, harmony, dissonance, and rhythm to operate outside the sounds of words and the audible patterns of meter. Its speaker has not yet ceased to sing in order to attempt simply to talk. Formally, the poem has yet to resist the easy intoxication of foreseeable rhyme. The energetic presence of silence has yet to be tapped.

Rather than cause for condemnation, I view such cases of mistaken identity as learning opportunities. They lead us back to poems—indeed, books of them—by poets who test and stretch our understanding of what a poem can do and be.

Nevertheless, if you still find yourself wondering or even insisting, *How do I know if a poem is good, and whether a poet is worth the limited resource of my time?* I get it. At this moment in human culture, we're encouraged to rate, rank, review, and doggedly defend or pithily dismiss most things and people in our midst. Often, we're rewarded for doing so swiftly and with verve. But what and whom does this habit serve? Does it make us experts? Does it prove anything that won't just as quickly be proven to the contrary? And isn't all this proving and disproving, this positing and pronouncing also, eventually, a tax on our energy and time? But go ahead, like something. This book has been organized around poems I hope might satisfy such an appetite. Recommend or even defend your choice to someone, if you need to. But please also carry with you the idea that a poem is an invitation to step outside this loop of habit and haste, and, for a time, to cease jockeying. It is an opportunity—temporary though it may be—to replace a system of worth based on power and capital with something else.

Poetry is a place writers go not to deposit meaning, but to seek it out.

ACKNOWLEDGMENTS

I conceived this book with the intention of writing an expansion of the lecture I delivered at the close of my first term as Poet Laureate of the United States, entitled "Staying Human: Poetry in the Age of Technology." But it eventually became clear to me that our collective relationship with digital technology has accelerated to such an extent since 2018 that the book such a topic warrants was one I no longer felt inclined to research, nor particularly qualified to write. Instead, I found my way into this meditation on poetry as a counterpoint to the larger value system of which technology is but one efficient vehicle.

And so I'd like to express immense and ongoing gratitude to Dr. Carla Hayden, the Librarian of Congress who changed my relationship to poetry and to America by inviting me to bring the art form that I love into vigorous engagement with my understanding of citizenship. My life was transformed utterly, and beautifully, by the revelations of that time. In fact, this book as a whole is an extension of those two years as an ambassador for poetry.

I'd also like to express gratitude and admiration for the remarkable Poetry and Literature program staff with whom it was my honor to work: Rob Casper, Anya Creightney, and Anne Holmes; as well as Guy Lamolinara, the head of the Center for the Book; Shari Rosenstein Werb, the director of the Center for Learning, Literacy and Engagement; and Shawn Miller, official photographer at the Library of Congress.

As always, I'm grateful for the light, courage, and hope I find in conversations with friends and thought-partners, among them Jericho Brown, Tina Chang, Ama Codjoe, Robin Coste Lewis, Melissa McGill, Kevin Newbury, Mary O'Connor, Leila Ortiz, Roger Reeves, David Semanki, Robin Beth Schaer, Happi Smith-Schick, Gregory Spears, and Kevin Young. Thank you, Ron Charles, for agreeing to be my interlocutor on the evening of my closing lecture at the Library of Congress in 2018.

Passages in the chapter "Fear Less: A Poem Is a Tool for Careful Listening" reflect upon my time as Poet Laureate and the American Conversations project I undertook in that role, and were originally conceived as part of a lecture I delivered at the Library of Congress in 2019, a version of which was printed in *The Washington Post*. The discussion of poetry and consciousness in that same chapter began as a lecture given at the 2023 Sun Valley Writers' Conference. Other passages draw upon text originally authored for the Minnesota Public Radio podcast *The Slowdown*. I want to express my deep appreciation to Jennifer Lai and Tracy Mumford.

Portions of "Who Are You?: On Strangers and Others" were delivered as a public lecture at Harvard Radcliffe Institute in September 2024, during my time in residence there as a Susan S. and Kenneth L. Wallach Professor. The inspiration, care, generous community, and joyful solitude I encountered at Radcliffe fostered numerous realizations and facilitated the completion of this book. With special gratitude to Tomiko Brown-Nagin, Claudia Rizzini, Jimena Codina, Hyun Jin Yoo, Allison Ney, and fellows Gabeba Baderoon, Lisa A. Crooms-Robinson, Tracey E. Hucks, Daniel

Immerwahr, Kelly Irwin, Aruni Kashyap, Akil Kumarasamy, Sonal Khullar, Claire Luchette, Yxta Maya Murray, Daphna Renan, and Sandra Susan Smith—and of course to Susan and Ken Wallach.

I also want to express gratitude, from myself and my students, for Victoria Adukwei Bulley's luminous and inspiring visit to Harvard in the spring of 2024.

Thank you, John Freeman and Jeff Shotts, for the encouragement of your friendship and belief.

Thank you to the remarkable team of professionals with whom I'm privileged to work and who made the delivery of this book possible: Jill Bialosky, Nicole Aragi, Kelsey Day, Markus Hoffmann, Eliza Fischer, Steven Barclay, and Sol Kim-Bentley.

And thank you—always and for everything—to Raf.

APPENDIX OF POETS

FRANK BIDART's wide-ranging poems are at once poised and formally adventurous, driven by the complexity and the contradictions of human interiority. His long persona poem "Ellen West," based upon the early twentieth-century case of a thirty-three-year-old woman in treatment for anorexia nervosa, explores the feelings of desire, hope, and relentlessness of a woman struggling to live with and as herself. In briefer lyrics, Bidart employs evocative line breaks, spacing, and typographic choices to further inflect the pitch and tone of a speaker's voice. The speaker of "The Yoke" encapsulates the experience of grief via a long unpunctuated line that resists closure:

> I sleep and wake and sleep and wake and sleep and wake and

A former Chancellor of the Academy of American Poets, Bidart's honors are the Bollingen Prize in American Poetry, the Wallace Stevens Award of the Academy of American Poets, the Lila Wallace-Reader's Digest Writers' Award, the Morton Dauwen Zabel Award given by the American Academy of Arts and Letters, the Shelley Award from the Poetry Society of America, and a fellowship from the National Endowment for the Arts. His recent books include *Watching the Spring Festival* (2008); *Metaphysical Dog* (2013), which won the National Book Critics Circle Award and was a finalist for the National Book Award; and *Half-Light: Collected Poems 1965–2016*, which won the National Book Award and the Pulitzer Prize in Poetry.

The poems of **ELIZABETH BISHOP** (1911–1979) perform feats of observation and description that place the speaker firmly and concretely in the meticulously rendered material world. Yet these surfaces often lead to moments of vulnerable interiority and transcendence, as when the speaker in "At the

Fishhouses" projects her awareness into the water she has been observing, announcing: "If you tasted it, it would first taste bitter, / then briny, then surely burn your tongue." Bishop published just over a hundred poems in her lifetime, though her vigilant craft and lyrical wakefulness has influenced generations of poets.

GWENDOLYN BROOKS's (1917–2000) early poems depict everyday lives of Black Chicagoans in formally dexterous lines and stanzas, work that earned her the first Pulitzer Prize awarded to an African American for her book *Annie Allen* (1949). In the late 1960s, inspired by the Black Arts Movement, Brooks's work shifted in style and scope, employing free verse (nonmetrical, non-rhyming poetry) and drawing upon vernacular speech. She took up teaching poetry workshops to members of a Chicago street gang, The Blackstone Rangers, and aligned herself with a younger generation of poets, among them Haki R. Madhubuti, in writing poems of social and racial consciousness. From 1985 to 1986, Brooks served as the Consultant in Poetry to the Library of Congress, a position later renamed the Poet Laureate of the United States. Her many poems offer a dazzling repository of sound and image, as with the lines "Chaos in windy grays / through a red prairie" which conclude "The Last Quatrain of the Ballad of Emmett Till." Here is the full text of Brooks's poem for Paul Robeson:

Paul Robeson

That time
we all heard it,
cool and clear,
cutting across the hot grit of the day.
The major Voice.
The adult Voice
forgoing Rolling River,
forgoing tearful tale of bale and barge
and other symptoms of an old despond.
Warning, in music-words
devout and large,
that we are each other's
harvest:

we are each other's
business:
we are each other's
magnitude and bond.

VICTORIA ADUKWEI BULLEY is a poet, writer, and artist whose work has appeared widely in the *London Review of Books*, *LitHub*, *The Atlantic*, and other publications. In her poems, she speaks-into-being a space out of view of the diminishing gaze by which Black life is too often grazed and held. She is the winner of an Eric Gregory Award, and her critically acclaimed debut poetry collection, *Quiet*, won the Folio Prize for poetry, the John Pollard Foundation International Poetry Prize, and was shortlisted for the T. S. Eliot Prize. *Quiet* is published by Faber & Faber in the UK and in North America by Knopf, Penguin Random House.

THOMAS CHATTERTON (1752–1770) was born in provincial Bristol, England, and wrote his first poem at ten years old; at eleven, he composed an eclogue (pastoral poem) called "Elinoure and Juga" and inscribed it onto parchment, claiming it was by Thomas Rowley, an entirely fictitious fifteenth-century monk. Subsequent Rowley poems gained wide acclaim, though they scared away potential patrons who suspected Rowley to be a hoax. Chatterton tried living by his pen, composing a comic opera, satires, and political tracts. He moved to London, slipped into starvation, and at age seventeen took his own life. In death, Chatterton grew into a mythic figure for generations of poets who saw in him a spirit of tragic literary genius.

The poems of **COUNTEE CULLEN** (1903–1946) explore race, religion, and spirituality in the rhymed couplets and quatrains of traditional English poetry. Yet his greater subject is the marriage of these forms to his own racial identity. "What is Africa to me?" asks his most famous poem, "Heritage," which wonders how one "three centuries removed / From the scenes his fathers loved" can comprehend his American Blackness. Cullen also edited *Caroling Dusk* (1927), an influential anthology of Harlem Renaissance poets. In his later years, he taught languages and writing at the former Frederick Douglass Junior High School in New York City, where he mentored a young James Baldwin.

Poet and linguist **NATALIE DIAZ** sees love as operating at the center of her poetics. She describes her first book, *When My Brother Was an Aztec*

(2012), which won the American Book Award, as having been animated by the questions, "How do you love, and even sometimes unlove, a family member who is an addict? And how does that affect the ways the family loves one another?" Centering queer-experience, the poems making up her Pulitzer Prize–winning *Postcolonial Love Poem* (2020) seek to "hold the ways we've been hurt and the ways we've been erased, and also to hold in the other hand, simultaneously, the way we deserve love, our capacities for love, and all of the innovative ways we've managed to find to express that love to one another." Diaz is the recipient of a MacArthur Fellowship, a USA Fellowship Award, a Lannan Foundation Literary Fellowship, and a Native Arts and Cultures Foundation Artist Fellowship. She is Mojave and an enrolled member of the Gila River Indian Tribe.

EMILY DICKINSON (1830–1886) lived for years in relative seclusion and during her lifetime published scarcely ten of her nearly 1,800 poems, many of which she wrote by hand and sewed into homemade booklets, called fascicles. Yet far from the prim and retiring "belle of Amherst" or "Queen Recluse" into which she has been mythologized, her lyrics and letters reveal an explosive, playful, and sensual intelligence—something like the "Vesuvius at home" one poem's speaker describes herself to be. Dickinson's compressed lines and quatrains, punctuated throughout by her idiosyncratic dashes, crackle with metaphor, wit, allusiveness, and a harrowing sense of the nearness of both transcendence and oblivion. Reading Dickinson provides endless small miracles: "The Stillness in the Room / Was like the Stillness in the Air — / Between the Heaves of Storm —"

MARK DOTY's ten books of poems have been honored by the National Book Critics Circle Award, the Los Angeles Times Book Prize, the T. S. Eliot Prize, and the 2008 National Book Award for *Fire to Fire: New and Selected Poems*. He has also published five volumes of nonfiction prose, including *Dog Years*, a *New York Times* bestseller and winner of the Stonewall Book Award from the American Library Association; *Heaven's Coast*, winner of the PEN/Martha Albrand Award for First Nonfiction; and *The Art of Description: World into Word*, a handbook for writers. His hybrid of memoir and literary criticism, *What Is the Grass: Walt Whitman in My Life*, was one of the five best-reviewed memoirs of 2020. Doty has received a Whiting Writers' Award, a Lila Wallace-Reader's Digest Writers' Award, and fellowships from the National Endowment for the Arts, the Guggenheim Foundation, and the Ingram Merrill Foundation. He was the

John and Rebecca Moores Professor at the University of Houston, and Distinguished Professor at Rutgers University, and has taught as a Visiting Professor at Stanford, Princeton, Columbia, New York University, and the University of Iowa. He lives in the Hudson River Valley.

Poet, short story writer, and novelist **PAUL LAURENCE DUNBAR** (1872–1906) was born in Dayton, Ohio. From an early age, Dunbar distinguished himself as a student journalist and class poet, but finances prevented him from attending college. While working as an elevator operator, Dunbar self-published a collection of poems, *Oak and Ivy*, and sold copies to passengers. Rising to wider popularity and international acclaim after the publication of his second book, *Majors and Minors*, he commenced to give reading and speaking tours, even embarking on a six-month tour of England in 1897. Throughout his career, Dunbar's work written in dialect, such as his poems "Deserted Plantation" and "When Malindy Sings," garnered far and away the greatest attention, no matter that the great majority of his poetry and prose was written in standard English; this disparity was a source of conflict and disappointment for the poet in his lifetime. Dunbar enjoyed friendships with Orville Wright, Frederick Douglass, and poet James Whitcomb Riley. While in England he collaborated with musician Samuel Coleridge-Taylor.

ROBERT FROST (1874–1963) was born in San Francisco, California, though he wrote and set most of his poems in rural New England. He won four Pulitzer Prizes, read at President John F. Kennedy's inauguration in 1961, and was perhaps the best-known American poet of the twentieth century. Frost filled his poems with what he called "the sound of sense," or speech patterns gleaned from everyday life; yet he married these sounds to a range of literary forms, most notably sonnets and blank verse (unrhymed iambic pentameter), as in these lines describing new leaves in a forest: "They think too much of having shaded out / A few old pecker-fretted apple trees."

JOY HARJO is an internationally renowned poet, performer, and writer of the Muscogee (Creek) Nation and served three terms as the 23rd Poet Laureate of the United States. Harjo is the author of ten books of poetry, most recently *Weaving Sundown in a Scarlet Light*; *An American Sunrise*, which won a 2020 Oklahoma Book Award; and *Conflict Resolution for Holy Beings*, which was shortlisted for the Griffin Poetry Prize. In addition to poetry, she has published several award-winning children's books, prose collections, plays, and two memoirs, including *Crazy Brave*, which was awarded the PEN Center USA Literary Award and the American Book Award. Harjo has edited several anthologies, including *When the Light of the World Was Subdued, Our Songs Came Through—A Norton Anthology of Native Nations Poetry*, and has produced seven award-winning music albums, including *Winding Through the Milky Way*, for which she was awarded a NAMMY for Best Female Artist of the year. Her many honors include Poetry Society of America's 2024 Frost Medal, Yale's 2023 Bollingen Prize for American Poetry, the National Book Critics Circle Ivan Sandrof Lifetime Achievement Award, a 2022 National Humanities Medal, and the Ruth Lilly Prize for Lifetime Achievement from the Poetry Foundation, among others. Harjo has served as a Chancellor of the Academy of American Poets, Board of Directors Chair of the Native Arts and Cultures Foundation, and is the inaugural artist-in-residence for Tulsa's Bob Dylan Center. She lives on the Muscogee Nation Reservation in Oklahoma.

ROBERT HAYDEN (1913–1980) is often remembered for his poems containing history, including "The Ballad of Nat Turner," the sonnet "Frederick Douglass," and the long poem "Middle Passage." "Runagate Runagate" (the term is archaic for *runaway*) draws on folk songs and spirituals, reward posters and Biblical allusions to describe a man's flight from the south and the rise of Harriet Tubman, "woman of earth, whipscarred / a summoning, a shining." Hayden grew deeply invested in his faith, serving as editor of the Baha'i *World Order* magazine. He taught for decades at Fisk University and the University of Michigan and served as Consultant in Poetry to the Library of Congress, an office later to be renamed the Poet Laureate of the United States.

The lines of **JOHN KEATS** (1795–1821) are often lush, rich with images held in a winding syntax, as in these lines from "Ode on Melancholy": "No, no, go not to Lethe, neither twist / Wolf's-bane, tight-rooted, for its poisonous wine." Some contemporaries thought his style overwrought, sentimental, and overly abstract; they savaged him in reviews ("a boy of pretty abilities," one wrote). Later generations have found in his sonnets, odes, and epic poems like *Hyperion* (1820) a mercurial poet obsessed not only with beautiful surfaces, but also the sufficiency of language to capture and contain the heights of experience. Keats's career as a writer was brief—he died of tuberculosis at age twenty-six—yet his legacy stands as an ambitious poet of abstract emotion and a devoted beholder of nature.

FRANCISCO MÁRQUEZ is a poet from Maracaibo, Venezuela, born in Miami, Florida. His work can be found in the *Brooklyn Rail*, the *Narrative Magazine*, the *Yale Review*, and the *Best American Poetry 2021* anthology, among other publications. His work has received fellowships from Bread Loaf Writers' Conference, Tin House, The Poetry Project, Brooklyn Poets, and the Fine Arts Work Center in Provincetown. He holds a master of fine arts from the New York University Creative Writing Program, where he was a Goldwater Fellow. He is an Editorial Fellow at Library of America and lives in Brooklyn, New York.

EDNA ST. VINCENT MILLAY (1892–1950) was raised with her two sisters by a single mother in Camden, Maine. Precocious and outspoken, Millay published her first poems while still in high school and garnered a great deal of early attention when her poem "Renascence" was published in *The Lyric Year* anthology of 1920, the year before she enrolled at Vassar. A playwright, magnetic stage actress, and a larger-than-life personality who was open about her love affairs with men and women, Millay moved to New York City after graduating from college. A contemporary of Robert Frost, she enjoyed widespread fame and recognition for her work, and received the 1923 Pulitzer Prize in Poetry for her book *The Ballad of the Harp-Weaver*.

A California resident, **HARRYETTE MULLEN** was born in Alabama and grew up in Texas. Celebrated for its spare lyricism, nimbly allusive word play, and sharp-edged intelligence, Mullen's poetry explores themes of race, gender, and language itself. Mullen's poetic imagination makes much music and derives many forms of meaning from what she has described as "puns, equivoque, the 'double talk' of metaphor and simile." Mullen's recent books are *Regaining Unconsciousness* (Graywolf, 2025), *Her Silver-Tongued Companion* (Edinburgh University, 2024), and *Open Leaves/poems from earth* (Black Sunflowers, 2023). Others include *Recyclopedia*, winner of a PEN Beyond Margins Award, and *Sleeping with the Dictionary*, a finalist for a National Book Award, National Book Critics Circle Award, and Los Angeles Times Book Prize. A collection of essays and interviews, *The Cracks Between What We Are and What We Are Supposed to Be* (University of Alabama, 2012) received an Elizabeth Agee Award. Graywolf Press published *Urban Tumbleweed: Notes from a Tanka Diary* in 2013. Her poems, short stories, and essays are reprinted in over one hundred anthologies, including several published by Norton, Oxford, Cambridge, and Penguin. Her work appears in *Best of Callaloo* and was selected six times for *Best American Poetry*. She is a recipient of a Stephen E. Henderson Award, Jackson Poetry Prize, United States Artist Fellowship, Academy of American Poets Fellowship, Guggenheim Fellowship, Katherine Newman Award for Best Essay on Multi-Ethnic Literatures of the United States, and a Gertrude Stein Award in Innovative American Poetry. In 2024 she received a Lifetime Achievement Award from Furious Flower Poetry Center. In 2023 she was elected to the American Academy of Arts and Sciences. Her poems have been translated into Spanish, French, German, Italian, Portuguese, Polish, Swedish, Danish, Turkish, Greek, Bulgarian, Russian, Hungarian, Kyrgyz, and Vietnamese. She teaches American poetry, African American literature, and creative writing at UCLA.

Palestinian American poet **NAOMI SHIHAB NYE** received the Wallace Stevens Award from the Academy of American Poets and the Texas Writer Award in 2024. In his judge's citation, Academy of American Poets Chancellor Afaa Michael Weaver writes:

> Nye's commitment to hope establishes her as one of the most important poet ambassadors in our time, extending as she does the image of the American literary artist as global citizen. In supporting civility in all spaces, she echoes the concerns of William Stafford, an important influence. What her work would have us know, namely that only peace brings lasting peace, is what her grandmother and elders taught her as a child, the ubiquitous power of the beauty of simple things, the necessities of life that we must share if we are to endure.

Nye writes that she yearns for a world of dialogue and shared hopes, and grieves daily for horrific injustices committed against beautiful humans. Her numerous poetry collections, and books of poetry for children, include the recent titles *The Tiny Journalist* (2019), *Grace Notes* (2024), *Transfer* (2011), *19 Varieties of Gazelle* (2002), *Voices in the Air* (2018), *Everything Comes Next* (2020), and the novels for children *The Turtle of Oman* (2009) and *The Turtle of Michigan* (2022).

CLAUDIA RANKINE's poems in exploration of the effects of race upon the collective imagination have transformed and expanded the contemporary American lyric. Her commitment to dialogue around our most fraught topics informs her writing and literary citizenship across forms, from poems, essays, and plays to video collaborations and her co-stewardship of the Racial Imaginary Institute. Rankine is the author of five books of poetry, including *Citizen: An American Lyric* and *Don't Let Me Be Lonely: An American Lyric*; three plays, including *Help*, which premiered in March 2020 (The Shed, NYC), and *The White Card*, which premiered in February 2018 (ArtsEmerson / American Repertory Theater) and was published by Graywolf Press in 2019. Her recent collection of essays, *Just Us: An American Conversation*, was published by Graywolf Press in 2020. She is also the coeditor of several anthologies including *The Racial Imaginary: Writers on Race in the Life of the Mind*.

MATT RASMUSSEN's debut poetry collection, *Black Aperture*, bears witness to the suicide of a sibling with tenderness, vulnerability, and profound emotional resourcefulness. In the poem "Reverse Suicide," the tragedy is narrated in reverse, making the poem an impossible undoing of the irreversible, and an overwhelming outpouring of love. *Black Aperture* received the 2012 Walt Whitman Award from the Academy of American Poets, the Minnesota Book Award for Poetry, and was named a finalist for the National Book Award. Rasmussen has been awarded the Holmes National Poetry Prize and a Pushcart Prize, as well as grants and fellowships from the Bush Foundation, the Minnesota State Arts Board, the Corporation of Yaddo, the Loft Literary Center, the Jerome Foundation, Intermedia Arts, the Anderson Center in Red Wing, Minnesota, and the McKnight Foundation. He is also a cofounder of the independent poetry press Birds, LLC. He teaches at Gustavus Adolphus College and lives in Robbinsdale, Minnesota.

PATRICK ROSAL's poems mine the contradictions and conundrums operating at the intimate scales of self, family, and city, as well as those of nations, global history, and collective memory. His work sheds lyric light on power, grief, joy, and resilience. Rosal is the author of six books, among them *The Last Thing: New and Selected Poems*, winner of the William Carlos Williams Award, and *Brooklyn Antediluvian*, which won the Academy of American Poets Lenore Marshall Poetry Prize. With interests that span several disciplines, he has made hundreds of appearances in Europe, Africa, Asia, and throughout the Americas. He has received fellowships from the John Simon Guggenheim Memorial Foundation, the National Endowment for the Arts, the Fulbright Research Scholar program, New Jersey State Council on the Arts (NJSCA), and the Civitella Ranieri residency. Rosal is the inaugural Campus Director of the Institute for the Study of Global Racial Justice at Rutgers University-Camden and Distinguished Professor of English.

PERCY BYSSHE SHELLEY (1792–1822) was a socially radical, staunchly atheistic, and prolific essayist, dramatist, and poet closely associated with the circle of British Romantic writers that included Lord Byron, William Wordsworth, and the poet's own wife, Mary Shelley. Known today for anthologized lyrics such as "Ozymandias" and "Ode to the West Wind," he also composed longer, philosophically and politically engaged works—*Adonais* is a pastoral elegy for his friend John Keats, and the drama *Prometheus Unbound* retells Aeschylus's version of the classical myth in verse. Shelley's lines often seethe with visionary language and social urgency, making him a figure many have turned to in times of crisis.

A poet of remarkable craft, range, and courage, **DANEZ SMITH** is one of the most celebrated literary voices of their generation, and a world-renowned slam poet. They are the author of four poetry collections including *Homie*, *Don't Call Us Dead*, and *[insert] boy*. *Bluff*, published in 2024, emerges out of Smith's own reckoning with violence, cynicism, and the artist's responsibility to their community. It is an awakening out of critical pessimism and into hope, honesty, and the world-making capacity of the imagination. Smith has won the Forward Prize for Best Collection, the Minnesota Book Award in Poetry, the Lambda Literary Award for Gay Poetry, and the Kate Tufts Discovery Award. They have been a finalist for the NAACP Image Award in Poetry, the National Book Critics Circle Award, and the National Book Award. A member of the Dark Noise Collective, and former cohost of the Webby-nominated podcast *VS (Versus)*, Smith is the recipient of fellowships from the Poetry Foundation, Princeton University, United States Artists, the McKnight Foundation, the Montalvo Arts Center, Cave Canem, and the National Endowment for the Arts. They live in Minneapolis near their people.

ANNE SPENCER (1882–1975) lived her entire life in Virginia, though she came to be associated with the Harlem Renaissance when Alain Locke selected her work for inclusion in his seminal anthology *The New Negro: An Interpretation*. From 1923 to 1945, during the height of her publishing career as a poet, Spencer was employed as the librarian at the Washington, DC, Paul Laurence Dunbar High School, the first public high school for Black students in the United States. Her poems reflect her commitment to racial equality and her love of gardening. These two themes can be seen to interact in the images running through the poem "Creed," which opens:

> If my garden oak spares one bare ledge
> For a boughed mistletoe to grow and wedge;
> And all the wild birds this year should know
> I cherish their freedom to come and go;

SARA TEASDALE (1884–1933) was born in St. Louis, Missouri, where, as an adolescent, she was a founding member of The Potters, an informal collective of young female poets and artists. During her adult career, she maintained relationships with literary luminaries in Chicago and New York City, including Harriet Monroe of *Poetry* magazine and Harlem Renaissance impresario Vachel Lindsay, and published eight poetry collections, one posthumously. Her 1917 book *Love Songs* won the Columbia University Poetry Prize (which later became the Pulitzer Prize). Teasdale's deftly metrical and musical lyrics observe the natural world, human intimacy, and the nature of the self.

Pulitzer Prize–winner **NATASHA TRETHEWEY** served two terms as the 19th Poet Laureate of the United States (2012–2014). In his citation, Librarian of Congress James Billington wrote, "Her poems dig beneath the surface of history—personal or communal, from childhood or from a century ago—to explore the human struggles that we all face." Trethewey was the first Southerner to receive the honor since Robert Penn Warren, in 1986, and the first African American since Rita Dove, in 1993. Trethewey is the author of *Monument* (2018), which was longlisted for the 2018 National Book Award, a retrospective drawing together verse that delineates the stories of working class African American women, a mixed-race prostitute, one of the first Black Civil War regiments, mestizo and mulatto figures in casta paintings, Gulf Coast victims of Katrina; *Thrall* (2012), which *The Washington Post* called "a powerful, beautifully crafted book"; *Native Guard* (2007), for which she won the Pulitzer Prize; *Bellocq's Ophelia* (2002), named a Notable Book for 2003 by the American Library Association; and *Domestic Work* (2000), which was selected by Rita Dove as the winner of the inaugural Cave Canem Poetry Prize for the best first book by an African American poet and won both the 2001 Mississippi Institute of Arts and Letters book prize and the 2001 Lillian Smith Book Award for poetry. Trethewey is also the author of the poetry chapbook *Congregation* (2015) and the prose book *Beyond Katrina: A Meditation on the Mississippi Gulf*

Coast (2012), and she served as editor of *The Best American Poetry 2017*. In addition to her poetry, Trethewey is the author of two memoirs, *The House of Being* (2024) and *Memorial Drive* (2020).

JOHN YAU is a poet, art critic, fiction writer, and curator who has published more than fifty books across genres, and contributed to numerous visual collaborations with artists. His poetry maintains a lyric commitment to the sound and feeling of language as a container for consciousness, an engagement with poetic form, and a visual thinker's investment in the world as it is seen. Humor and play are also key components of Yau's verse, even in exploring the complexities of race and racialized identity in America. Recent books include *Disguise the Limit: John Yau's Collaborations* (2024), *Please Wait by the Coatroom: Reconsidering Race and Identity in American Art* (2023), *Tell It Slant* (2023), *Bijoux in the Dark* (2018), and *Further Adventures in Monochrome* (2012). Born in Lynn, Massachusetts, to Chinese emigrants, he is the founding editor of the small press *Black Square Editions* and Professor of Critical Studies at Rutgers University's Mason Gross School of the Arts. His work has been honored with the Jackson Poetry Prize; fellowships from the National Endowment for the Arts, the Ingram-Merrill Foundation, and the Guggenheim Foundation; and the Rabkin Prize for excellence in visual arts journalism. His books of art criticism include *In the Realm of Appearances: The Art of Andy Warhol* (1993) and *A Thing Among Things: The Art of Jasper Johns* (2009), as well as monographs on Wifredo Lam, Thomas Nozkowski, Joe Brainard, Catherine Murphy, A. R. Penck, Richard Artschwager, Pat Steir, Liu Xiaodong, and Kim Tschang-yeul.

NOTES

10 **"'Oh, my sweet mother, 't is in vain,"**: Sappho, "A Girl in Love," translated by Thomas Moore, *Masterpieces of Greek Literature*, edited by John Henry Wright (New York: Houghton Mifflin, 1902), 58.

16 **"Old Hogan's goat was feeling fine..."**: "Old Hogan's Goat" derives from an American folk song with numerous variants. It is also sometimes entitled "Old Grogan's Goat." The version adopted in this chapter is drawn from memory.

21 **"Sundays too my father got up early"**: Robert Hayden, "Those Winter Sundays," *Collected Poems of Robert Hayden*, edited by Frederick Glaysher (New York: Liveright, 1966), 41.

26 **"when man is capable of being in uncertainties"**: Letter to George and Tom Keats, 21, 27 (?) December 1817, *The Letters of John Keats, 1814–1821*, Vol. 2, edited by H. E. Rollins (Cambridge: Harvard University Press, 1958), 193.

26 **"more, / And still more"**: John Keats, "To Autumn," *Lamia, Isabella, The Eve of St Agnes, and Other Poems* (London: Taylor and Hessey, 1820), 138–39.

35 **"She had some horses. / She had horses who were bodies of sand."**: Joy Harjo, "She Had Some Horses," *She Had Some Horses: Poems* (New York: W. W. Norton, 2008), 61–63.

40 **"She had horses with long, pointed breasts"**: Joy Harjo, "She Had Some Horses," *She Had Some Horses* (New York: Thunder's Mouth Press, 1983), 64.

43 **"the poet's work to reduce the poem"**: Joy Harjo, "Introduction," *She Had Some Horses: Poems* (New York: W. W. Norton, 2008), ix.

43 **"Like most poets, I don't really"**: Harjo, "Introduction," x.

43 **"I understand there was some exchange"**: Harjo, "Introduction."

44 **"And there was the horse that came to see me":** Harjo, "Introduction."
44 **"A human being is a part of the whole":** Albert Einstein, condolence letter to Norman Salit, March 4, 1950, *The New Quotable Einstein*, edited by Alice Calaprice (Princeton University Press, 2005), 206.
47 **". . . who climbed in her / bed":** Joy Harjo, *She Had Some Horses* (New York: Thunder's Mouth Press, 1983), 64.
48 **"space not defined or bound":** Joy Harjo, "Introduction," *She Had Some Horses: Poems* (New York: W. W. Norton, 2008), ix.
52 **"Wrapped in gold foil, in the search":** Mark Doty, "Ararat" in *Bethlehem in Broad Daylight* (Boston: David R. Godine, 1991), 21.
57 **"a momentary stay against confusion":** Robert Frost, "The Figure a Poem Makes," *Complete Poems of Robert Frost* (New York: Holt, Rinehart, and Winston, 1939), vi.
58 **"For me the initial delight is in the surprise":** Frost, "The Figure a Poem Makes," vi.
59 **"We enjoy the straight crookedness":** Frost, "The Figure a Poem Makes," vii.
60 **"May what you have made descend upon you.":** Frank Bidart, "Curse," *Half-Light: Collected Poems 1965–2016* (New York: Farrar, Straus and Giroux, 2017), 361.
63 **"we were kindergarten sweethearts.":** Danez Smith, "rose," *Homie* (Minneapolis: Graywolf Press, 2020), 13.
69 **"the damage done to one's conscience":** "What Is Moral Injury," The Moral Injury Project at Syracuse University, October 9, 2024.
72 **"Why and by whose power were you sent?":** Tracy K. Smith, "The United States Welcomes You," *Wade in the Water* (Minneapolis: Graywolf Press, 2018), 41.
77 **"Where did the power go?":** Naomi Shihab Nye, "My Wisdom," *The Tiny Journalist* (Rochester, NY: BOA Editions, 2019), 53.
82 **"I've been working on the railroad / All the livelong day!":** "I've Been Working on the Railroad," a derivation of "Levee Song," dates back to 1894.
86 **"Two hundred metres down, the light stops.":** Victoria Adukwei Bulley, "The Ultra-Black Fish," *Quiet* (New York: Knopf, 2022), 61.
94 **"He has / sent hither swarms of Officers to harass our people":** Tracy K. Smith, "Declaration," *Wade in the Water* (Minneapolis: Graywolf Press, 2018), 19.
97 **"Oh, sinner man, where you gonna run to?":** "Oh Sinner Man" and

"Sinnerman" are variants of a traditional nineteenth-century African American spiritual. Popular twentieth-century arrangements have been recorded by artists Nina Simone and Les Baxter.

98 **"We are not responsible for your lost or stolen relatives."**: Harryette Mullen, "We Are Not Responsible," *Sleeping with the Dictionary* (Berkeley: University of California Press, 2002), 77.

101 **widely reproduced online as a lineated five-stanza poem:** Harryette Mullen, "We Are Not Responsible," Poetry Foundation website.

104 **"Political language—and with variations"**: George Orwell, "Politics and the English Language," *Horizon* 13, no. 76 (1946): 252–65.

107 **"I love you freely."**: Abraham Lincoln papers at the Library of Congress: Series 1. General Correspondence, 1833–1916: Mrs. Luther Fowler [George Washington] to Abraham Lincoln, Sunday, March 19, 1865. (Writes on behalf of freedman at Hilton Head.)

108 **"I would be glad to go back"**: Lincoln papers, Series 1.

110 **"we are each other's"**: Gwendolyn Brooks, "Paul Robeson," *Family Pictures* (Detroit: Broadside Press, 1970), 19.

111 **"Mr abarham lincon"**: Jane Welcome to Abraham Lincoln, November 21, 1864; File W-934-CT-1864; Letters Received, Colored Troops Division, 1863–1888; Records of the Adjutant General's Office, Record Group 94; National Archives Building, Washington, DC. The reply sent to Welcom states that "the interests of the service will not permit that your request be granted.": C. W. Foster to Jane Welcome, December 2, 1864; File W-934-CT-1864; LR, Colored Troops Division, 1863–1888; Records of the Adjutant General's Office, RG 94; NAB, Washington, DC.

112 **while conducting research for a poem commissioned:** My poem "I Will Tell You the Truth About This, I Will Tell You All About It" was originally published in the exhibition catalog *Lines in Long Array: A Civil War Commemoration, Poems and Photographs, Past and Present*, edited by David C. Ward and Frank H. Goodyear III (Washington, DC: Smithsonian Institution Press, 2013). The poem is also included in my collection *Wade in the Water: Poems* (Minneapolis: Graywolf Press, 2018).

115 **"I often feel unsure or unsatisfied"**: Francisco Márquez, "Contributors' Notes and Comments," *Best American Poetry 2021*, edited by David Lehman and Tracy K. Smith (New York: Scribner, 2021), 194.

116 **"Fixed at sunset, a wooden blue shack"**: Francisco Márquez, "Provincetown," *The Common* 20 (October 28, 2020).

123 **"I shall gather myself into myself again,":** Sara Teasdale, "The Crystal Gazer," *Dark of the Moon* (New York: The Macmillan Company, 1926), 57.
127 **"I had forgotten how the frogs must sound":** Edna St. Vincent Millay, "Assault," *Collected Poems* (New York: Book-of-the-Month Club, 1990), 77.
132 **"You grow up hearing two languages. Neither fits your fits":** John Yau, "Music from Childhood," *Bijoux in the Dark* (Tucson and Seattle: Letter Machine Editions, 2018), 21.
138 **"We tell the story every year—":** Natasha Trethewey, "Incident," *Native Guard* (Boston: Houghton Mifflin Company, 2006), 41.
144 **"Ah, how poets sing and die!":** Anne Spencer, "Dunbar," *The Book of American Negro Poetry*, edited by James Weldon Johnson (New York: Harcourt, Brace, and Co., 1922), 174.

CREDITS

21 **"Those Winter Sundays"**: "Those Winter Sundays." Copyright © 1966 by Robert Hayden, from *Collected Poems of Robert Hayden* by Robert Hayden, edited by Frederick Glaysher. Used by permission of Liveright Publishing.

35 **"She Had Some Horses"**: "She Had Some Horses." Copyright © 1983 by Joy Harjo, from *She Had Some Horses* by Joy Harjo. Copyright © 2008, 1983 by Joy Harjo. Used by permission of W. W. Norton & Company, Inc.

42 **Introduction to the 2008 reissue of *She Had Some Horses* (excerpts)**: "Introduction," from *She Had Some Horses* by Joy Harjo. Copyright © 2008, 1983 by Joy Harjo. Used by permission of W. W. Norton & Company, Inc.

44 **Condolence letter to Norman Salit (excerpt)**: Albert Einstein, "Condolence Letter to Norman Salit," from *The Collected Papers of Albert Einstein*. Copyright © 1987 by Princeton University Press. Reprinted with the permission of Copyright Clearance Center, Inc., on behalf of Princeton University Press.

52 **"Ararat"**: Mark Doty, "Ararat," from *Paragon Park: Turtle, Swan; Bethlehem in Broad Daylight; Early Poems*. Copyright © 2012 by Mark Doty. Reprinted with the permission of The Permissions Company, LLC, on behalf of David R. Godine, Publisher, Inc.

57 **"The Figure a Poem Makes" (excerpt)**: Excerpts from "The Figure a Poem Makes," by Robert Frost, from *The Selected Prose of Robert Frost*, edited by Hyde Cox and Edward Connery Lathem. Copyright © 1923, 1969 by Henry Holt and Company. Copyright © 1951 by Robert Frost. Reprinted by permission of Henry Holt and Company. All Rights Reserved.

172 CREDITS

60 **"Curse" (excerpt):** Excerpt from "Curse," from *Half-Light: Collected Poems 1965–2016*, by Frank Bidart. Copyright © 2017 by Frank Bidart. Reprinted by permission of Farrar, Straus and Giroux. All Rights Reserved.

63 **"rose":** Danez Smith, "rose," from *Homie*. Copyright © 2020 by Danez Smith. Reprinted with the permission of The Permissions Company, LLC, on behalf of Graywolf Press, graywolfpress.org.

72 **"The United States Welcomes You":** Tracy K. Smith, "The United States Welcomes You," from *Such Color: New and Selected Poems*. Copyright © 2018 by Tracy K. Smith. Reprinted with the permission of The Permissions Company, LLC, on behalf of Graywolf Press, graywolfpress.org.

77 **"My Wisdom" (excerpt):** Naomi Shahib Nye, excerpt from "My Wisdom" from *The Tiny Journalist*. Copyright © 2019 by Naomi Shihab Nye. Reprinted with the permission of The Permissions Company, LLC, on behalf of BOA Editions, Ltd., boaeditions.org.

81 **260 "[I'm Nobody...]":** *The Poems of Emily Dickinson: Variorum Edition*, edited by Ralph W. Franklin, Cambridge, Mass.: The Belknap Press of Harvard University Press, Copyright © 1998 by the President and Fellows of Harvard College. Copyright © 1951, 1955 by the President and Fellows of Harvard College. Copyright © renewed 1979, 1983 by the President and Fellows of Harvard College. Copyright © 1914, 1918, 1919, 1924, 1929, 1930, 1932, 1935, 1937, 1942 by Martha Dickinson Bianchi. Copyright © 1952, 1957, 1958, 1963, 1965 by Mary L. Hampson. Used by permission. All rights reserved.

86 **"The Ultra-Black Fish":** "The Ultra-Black Fish" from *Quiet: Poems* by Victoria Adukwei Bulley, copyright © 2022 by Victoria Adukwei Bulley. Used by permission of Alfred A. Knopf, an imprint of the Knopf Doubleday Publishing Group, a division of Penguin Random House LLC. All rights reserved.

94 **"Declaration":** Tracy K. Smith, "Declaration," from *Such Color: New and Selected Poems*. Copyright © 2018 by Tracy K. Smith. Reprinted with the permission of The Permissions Company, LLC, on behalf of Graywolf Press, graywolfpress.org.

98 **"We Are Not Responsible":** "We Are Not Responsible," from *Sleeping with the Dictionary* by Harryette Mullen, © 2002 by The Regents of the

University of California, used with permission of the University of California Press.

110 **"Paul Robeson":** "Paul Robeson" by Gwendolyn Brooks, reprinted by consent of Brooks Permissions.

115 **"Provincetown":** "Provincetown" and excerpt from "About this Poem" appear by permission of Francisco Márquez.

132 **"Music from Childhood":** "Music From Childhood," from *Bijoux in the Dark*, published in 2018 by Letter Machine Editions appears by permission of John Yau.

138 **"Incident":** "Incident," from *Native Guard* by Natasha Trethewey. Copyright © 2006 by Natasha Trethewey. Used by permission of HarperCollins Publishers.

INDEX

abstraction, 20, 76, 131
addressees, in poems, 26n, 71–76, 93, 99–100, 104, 131
agency, 70–71, 89
Alzheimer's disease, 9
ambiguity, 20, 26, 41, 100
American Book Award, 158, 160
American Conversations project, Library of Congress, 6–10
American Journal (anthology), 7, 9
American politics
    America as divided, 5–14, 33, 61–62, 112, 119
    citizenship, 41, 45–46, 62, 71, 88, 95, 100
    election of 2016, 6
    political language, 104
    September 11, 2001, attacks, 60
    See also community; United States
anaphora, 39
"Ararat" (Doty), 52–57, 59–60
Arbery, Ahmaud, 88
"Assault" (Millay), 126–30
audiences. *See* reading poetry
authors. *See* writing poetry
Ayyad, Janna Jihad, 77

Baldwin, James, 157
Ballad of the Harp-Weaver, The (Millay), 161
"Be ye not afraid," 122
beauty, 4, 45, 127–29, 144–49

belonging, 5, 42, 46–47, 66–67, 99–100
Bible, the, 18, 22, 109, 122n
Bidart, Frank, 60–62, 155
Billington, James, 165
Bishop, Elizabeth, 5, 155–56
Black Aperture (Rasmussen), 163
Black Arts Movement, 156
Black people, 8, 95, 142, 143
    African American dialect, 146, 159
    letters to Lincoln, 106–14
    slavery, 83, 96–97, 100–101, 106–12, 144–46
    stereotypes about, 82–83, 86–90, 96–97, 103
    violence against, 70, 71–76
blank verse, 159
Brooks, Gwendolyn, 5, 110–11, 156–57
Brown v. Board of Education, 8
Bulley, Victoria Adukwei, 86–91, 106, 157

"Camptown Races" (minstrel song), 83n
Caroling Dusk (anthology), 157
Chatterton, Thomas, 144, 146–47, 157
children, 7–8, 15–19, 50, 66, 82–83
citizenship, 41, 45–46, 62, 71, 88, 95, 100
Civil War, 112–14, 118–19
clickbait, 33

closure, 24, 143–48
cognitive failure, 117
collective imagination, 5, 66, 75, 91–93, 101–3
community, 6–7
   belonging to, 5, 42, 46–47, 66–67, 99–100
   careful listening, 1–14, 17–18, 49, 61–62, 80, 92–93, 105, 115, 134
   children, 7–8, 15–19, 50, 66, 82–83
   collective imagination, 5, 66
   common reality, 30, 91–92, 96–98, 105, 108–11, 113
   estrangement, 47–48
   fear and the limits of obligation, 98–99
   the freight of history carried through, 5, 32, 47, 51, 54, 62, 66, 72, 95, 100, 142
   group allegiance, 66–67
   older members, 9
   strangers among us, 2–3, 10, 13, 32–33, 81–114
   See also distance
consciousness, 44–45
   introspection, 2, 25–26
   intuition, 12, 19, 48, 58, 67
   perception, 2, 26, 29, 48, 67–68, 88–90
   poetry as redeeming act, 115–19
   the work of the unconscious, 18–22, 25, 27, 43, 86, 142
   See also self, the
"contrabands," 106
"Creed" (Spencer), 165
"Crystal Gazer, The" (Teasdale), 123–26
Cullen, Countee, 142, 157
curiosity, 19–20
"Curse" (Bidart), 60–62

dactyls, 146–47
dashes, 81, 85–86, 95
"Declaration" (T. K. Smith), 93–96
Declaration of Independence, 92–96

dialect, African American, 146, 159
Diallo, Amadou, 99
Diaz, Natalie, 5, 157–58
Dickinson, Emily, 81–86, 106, 118–19, 158
distance, 3–4, 18–19
   psychic distance, 73
   between public and private, 45
   of social status, 108
   of time, 113, 121
Doty, Mark, 52–60, 158–59
Dove, Rita, 165
"Dunbar" (Spencer), 144–48
Dunbar, Paul Laurence, 144–48, 159

eclogues (pastoral poems), 157
Einstein, Albert, 44–46
elegies, 52–56
emotions
   feeling small, 2–3
   grief, 12–13, 19, 30–32, 50–60, 68, 134
   hatred, 4, 105
   indifference, 22–23
   love, 1, 10, 18–19, 21, 24–25, 37, 41, 43–49
   moral injury, 68–71
   safety, 55, 66–67, 72, 78–79, 98, 130
   See also fear
empathy, 12, 19, 24–25, 32–33, 67, 83, 106, 127, 140
end-stopped lines, 101–2, 140
epics, 10
erasure, 86, 91–96, 106, 134
estrangement, 47–48

fear, 1–4, 5, 12, 18–19, 46
   "Be ye not afraid," 122
   how we carry, 128
   inaction and helplessness, 69–71
   and the limits of obligation, 98–99
   misidentifying the violence around us, 76–77, 80
   the opposite of love, 4
   of poetry, 3–4, 120–51

"Figure a Poem Makes, The" (Frost), 57–59, 76
first-person point of view, 99–100, 126, 139
Floyd, George, 88
form, 11, 25, 135–43
   blank verse, 159
   eclogues (pastoral poems), 157
   elegies, 52–56
   end-stopped lines, 101–2, 140
   epics, 10
   found poems, 87n
   lyric poetry, 10, 26n, 135, 150
   odes, 26–27
   pantoum, 131, 135–39, 143
   persona poems, 146, 155
   prose poems, 64, 98–99
   sonnets, 25, 71–76, 159
   stanzaic patterns, 137
   white space, 129, 137–38, 141–42
   See also meter
forms of address, 71–76, 93
found poems, 87n
Frost, Robert, 57–59, 76, 159

gaze, 75, 86, 117, 157
"Girl in Love, A" (Sappho), 10–11
"great poetry." *See* judgment
grief, 12–13, 19, 30–32, 50–60, 68, 134
group allegiance, 66–67

Harjo, Joy, 34–49, 159–60
Harlem Renaissance, 142, 157, 164, 165
Hayden, Carla, 5
Hayden, Robert, 5, 21–26, 160
history, 5, 32, 47, 51, 54, 62, 66, 72, 95, 100, 142
Homie (D. Smith), 70

"I Will Tell You the Truth About This, I Will Tell You All About It," 114n
"[I'm Nobody! Who Are You]" (Dickinson), 81–86, 106, 118–19, 158
"I've been working on the railroad," 82–83
images, 2–3, 11, 18, 20–23, 29–31, 38–42, 131–35
imagination, collective, 5, 66, 75, 91–93, 101–3
imagination, individual, 2–6, 30, 31, 5, 66, 131–35
"Incident" (Cullen), 142
"Incident" (Trethewey), 138–43
indifference, 22–23
internal rhyme, 40, 75–76
introspection, 2, 25–26
intuition, 12, 19, 48, 58, 67

Jefferson, Thomas, 92–96
"Jimmy Crack Corn" (minstrel song), 83n
judgment of poetry, 13, 148–51

"Karens," 87–89
Keats, John, 26–31, 39, 144–47, 160
"Keep calm and carry on," 122
Ku Klux Klan, 139

language, 2, 5, 13, 43, 79, 96, 120
   abstraction, 20, 76, 131
   ambiguity, 20, 26, 41, 100
   deliberately false, 104
   dialect, 146, 159
   dual-language households, 132–34
   everyday language, 120–22
   failures of, 76
   literary English, 146
   musical behavior of, 22, 56
   our relationship to, 48–51
   platitudes, 25, 28
   political language, 104
   See also images; poetic device; sounds
Lee, William "Billy," 108
Library of Congress
   American Conversations project, 6–10

Consultants in Poetry of the, 156, 160
Poet Laureates of the United States, 5–14, 156, 159, 160, 165
Lincoln, Abraham, letters to, 106–14
listening carefully, 1–14, 17–18, 49, 61–62, 80, 92–93, 105, 115, 134
literary devices. *See* poetic devices
Locke, Alain, 164
lyric poetry, 10, 26n, 135, 150

Madhubuti, Haki R., 156
Majors and Minors (Dunbar), 159
Make America Great Again!, 98
"mankind's optical delusion," 44–45
Márquez, Francisco, 115–18, 161
Memorial Drive: A Daughter's Memoir (Trethewey), 142
memory, 2, 12, 18–22, 41–44, 53–55, 65, 102, 127–29, 131, 133–35
metaphor, 20, 30, 43, 58, 64, 109
meter, 15, 75–76, 137, 145–47, 150
  blank verse, 159
  falling vs. rising, 145
  metrical feet, 73, 145–47
  quatrains, 136–41
  See also time
Millay, Edna St. Vincent, 126–30, 161
Ministry of Information (UK), 122n
minstrelsy, 82–83
moral injury, 68–71
Mullen, Harryette, 98–106, 161–62
Muscogee (Creek) people, 40–41, 160
"Music from Childhood" (Yau), 131–35, 135–39, 143
musical behavior of language, 22, 56
"My Wisdom" (Nye), 76–80

National Book Award, 155, 158, 161, 163, 164, 165
National Portrait Gallery, Washington, DC, 112
Native American cultures, 40–41
Negative Capability, 26

New Negro: An Interpretation, The (anthology), 164
"Nobodyness," 83–84, 92, 106
Nye, Naomi Shihab, 76–80, 162

Oak and Ivy (Dunbar), 159
odes, 26–27
"Oh, Sinner Man" (spiritual), 96–97, 168–69
"Old Dan Tucker" (minstrel song), 83n
"Old Hogan's Goat" (folk song), 15–19, 167
Orwell, George, 104

Palestine, 77
pantoum, 131, 135–39, 143
"Paul Robeson" (Brooks), 110–11, 156–57
PEN Center USA Literary Award, 160
perception, 2, 26, 29, 48, 67–68, 88–90
persona poems, 146, 155
personas, 124–25. *See also* speaker, the
personhood, 106. *See* "nobody"
platitudes, 25, 28
poems
  acts of attention, 49
  acts of reckoning, 24, 56, 85, 115
  like cars, 2
  invitations to an encounter, 121
  mothers to many, 6
  like pumpkin flowers, 113
  like raucous herds, 34
  see you and wave, 15
  like undertaking a trust-fall, 6
Poet Laureates of the United States, 5–14, 156, 159, 160, 165
poetic device
  anaphora, 39
  metaphor, 20, 30, 43, 58, 64, 109
  repetition, 19, 24, 39, 42, 65, 78, 131, 136–38, 150

poetic device (*continued*)
  rhyme, 15, 28, 40, 75–76, 85, 136–41, 150
  simile, 20, 64
  See also form; meter; sounds
poetry, 1–14
  beauty in, 4, 45, 127–29, 144–49
  a brief guide to, 120–51
  children's poetry and songs, 15–19, 82–83
  closure in, 24, 143–48
  defining a poem, 120–22
  erasure in, 86, 91–96, 106, 134
  fear of, 3–4
  getting us to community, 6–7
  Harlem Renaissance, 142, 157, 164, 165
  judging, 148–51
  as not formulaic, 11
  as redeeming act, 115–19
  Romantic Movement, 26, 146
  the sensory dimension of, 20–22, 84, 128–29
  as technology of careful listening, 1–14, 17–18, 49, 61–62, 80, 92–93, 105, 115, 134
  the title of a poem, 126–30
  why it matters, 31–34
  the work of the unconscious, 15–49
politics. *See* American politics; community; language
Port Royal, Battle of, 106
Postcolonial Love Poem (Diaz), 160
post-traumatic stress disorder, 69
power, 42–43, 46–49, 62, 72–73, 75–79, 84, 151
privilege, 97, 100, 105
prose poems, 64, 98–99
prosody, 145–47
"Provincetown" (Márquez), 115–18
psychology, 69
Pulitzer Prize in Poetry, 155, 156, 159, 161, 165
punctuation, 85–86, 101–2, 136, 140
  dashes, 81, 85–86, 95

quatrains, 136–41
quiet. *See* silence

race and racism, 6, 82–83, 89, 95, 142
Rankine, Claudia, 5, 162–63
rape, 47
Rasmussen, Matt, 9, 163
reading poetry, 1–14
  aloud, 5, 11, 16–17, 139, 145
  a brief guide to, 120–51
  as co-creation, 31–34
  identifying the addressee, 26n, 71–76, 93, 99–100, 104, 131
  matters of taste, 148–49
  See also form; poetic device; speaker, the
reality in common, 30, 91–92, 96–98, 105, 108–11, 113
repetition, 19, 24, 39, 42, 65, 78, 131, 136–38, 150
"Reverse Suicide" (Rasmussen), 9
rhyme, 15, 28, 40, 75–76, 85, 136–41, 150
Romanticism, 26, 146
Rosal, Patrick, 5, 163–64
"Rose" (D. Smith), 62–68
rupture of the self, 34, 44, 48, 86

safety, 55, 66–67, 72, 78–79, 98, 130
Sappho, 10–11
"scatterbrain," 123–24
second-person point of view, 99–100, 131
self, the, 1–4, 10
  agency, 70–71, 89
  the material self, 2
  memory and, 2, 12, 18–22, 41–44, 53–55, 65, 102, 127–29, 131, 133–35
  rupture of, 34, 44, 48, 86
  versions of the self, 67, 121
  wilderness within, 34
  See also consciousness

sensory dimension, 20–22, 84, 128–29
perception, 2, 26, 29, 48, 67–68, 88–90
See also memory; poetic device; sounds
September 11, 2001, attacks, 60
"She Had Some Horses" (Harjo), 34–49
Shelley, Percy Bysshe, 146–47, 164
silence, in our lives, 9, 17, 51
silence, in poems, 37, 64, 76–81, 82, 95, 103, 127–29, 141, 142, 145, 150
similes, 20, 64
slavery, 83, 96–97, 100–101, 106–12, 144–46
Smith, Danez, 62–68, 70, 164
Smith, Tracy K., 1–14
  American Conversations project, 6–10
  as a child reciting poetry, 15–19
  in college, 2–3
  "Declaration," 92–96
  on Emily Dickinson, 81–86
  encounter with police, 74
  in high school, 66
  loss of her mother, 50–52
  as Poet Laureate of the United States, 5–14
  reading practice of, 12, 30
  "The United States Welcomes You," 71–76
songs, 4, 10, 16, 147, 150
  birdsong, 53–55, 143
  children's songs, 82–83
  "how poets sing and die," 144–47
  "songs of spring," 27–31
  spirituals, 96–97
sonnets, 25, 71–76, 159
sounds, 2–3, 11, 22, 43, 150
  dialect, 146, 159
  musical behavior of language, 22, 56
  reading poetry out loud, 5, 11, 16–17, 139, 145

silence in our lives, 9, 17, 51
silence in poems, 37, 64, 76–81, 82, 95, 103, 127–29, 141, 142, 145, 150
sound-based images, 134
speaker, the, 1, 10–11, 13, 23–24, 123–26
  first-person point of view, 99–100, 126, 139
  forms of address, 71–76, 93
  gazing inward, 117
  second-person point of view, 99–100, 131
  speaking to addressees, 26n, 71–76, 93, 99–100, 104, 131
Spencer, Anne, 144–48, 164–65
strangers, 2–3, 10, 13, 32–33, 81–114. *See also* speaker, the

taste, 148–49
Taylor, Breonna, 88
Teasdale, Sara, 123–26, 165
technology, 4, 7, 32–33, 70
  poetry as technology of careful listening, 1–14, 17–18, 49, 61–62, 80, 92–93, 105, 115, 134
The Potters (informal collective), 165
"Those Winter Sundays" (Hayden), 21–26
time
  delusion of linear time, 44–49
  distance through, 19, 31, 35–37
  marking time in poetry, 21–22
  slowing down, 2–4
  See also meter
Tiny Journalist, The (Nye), 77
"To Autumn" (Keats), 26–31
tools. *See* technology
Trethewey, Natasha, 138–39, 142–43, 165–66
Twitter, 30

"Ultra-Black Fish, The" (Bulley), 86–91, 106
unconscious, the, 15–49, 86, 142

United States
  Civil War, 112–14, 118–19
  Declaration of Independence, 92–96
  myth of a divided nation, 5–14, 33, 61–62, 112, 119
  Native American cultures, 40–41
  race and racism, 6, 82–83, 89, 95, 142
  See also American culture
"United States Welcomes You, The" (T. K. Smith), 71–76
"Untitled" poems, 126
"Urban Youth," 66
US Army, 106
US Supreme Court, 8

violence, 33, 47, 61, 70–71, 75–76, 105, 130

warfare, 10, 41, 62, 79, 101, 109
  Civil War, 112–14, 118–19
  experience of Black soldiers, 106–10, 112–14

Warren, Robert Penn, 165
Washington, George, of South Carolina, 106–10
"We Are Not Responsible" (Mullen), 98–106
Weaver, Afaa Michael, 162
Welcom, Jane, 111–14, 169
When My Brother Was an Aztec (Diaz), 157–58
white people, 63, 65, 83, 87–89, 97, 100, 102–3, 106
white space, 129, 137–38, 141–42
women, 47, 87–89, 123–25
writing poetry, 8, 43, 57–58, 75–77, 92–94, 115, 121–22, 148–51
  an author's intentions, 12
  beyond the frame of one's singular experience, 10–11
  a place writers go not to deposit meaning, 151
  a poem's intention, 2
  research, 112–13

Yau, John, 131–35, 135–39, 143, 166

Norton Shorts

BRILLIANCE WITH BREVITY

W. W. Norton & Company has been independent since 1923, when William Warder Norton and Mary (Polly) D. Herter Norton first published lectures delivered at the People's Institute, the adult education division of New York City's Cooper Union. In the 1950s, Polly Norton transferred control of the company to its employees.

One hundred years after its founding, W. W. Norton & Company inaugurates a new century of visionary independent publishing with Norton Shorts. Written by leading-edge scholars, these eye-opening books deliver bold thinking and fresh perspectives in under two hundred pages.

Available Fall 2025

    Imagination: A Manifesto by Ruha Benjamin

    What's Real about Race?: Untangling Science, Genetics, and Society by Rina Bliss

    Offshore: Stealth Wealth and the New Colonialism by Brooke Harrington

    Sex Beyond "Yes": Pleasure and Agency for Everyone by Quill R Kukla

    Fewer Rules, Better People: The Case for Discretion by Barry Lam

    Explorers: A New History by Matthew Lockwood

    Wild Girls: How the Outdoors Shaped the Women Who Challenged a Nation by Tiya Miles

    The Trafficker Next Door: How Household Employers Exploit

Domestic Workers by Rhacel Salazar Parreñas

The Moral Circle: Who Matters, What Matters, and Why by Jeff Sebo

Against Technoableism: Rethinking Who Needs Improvement by Ashley Shew

Fear Less: Poetry in Perilous Times by Tracy K. Smith

Literary Theory for Robots: How Computers Learned to Write by Dennis Yi Tenen

Forthcoming

Mehrsa Baradaran on the racial wealth gap

Merlin Chowkwanyun on the social determinants of health

Daniel Aldana Cohen on eco-apartheid

Jim Downs on cultural healing

Reginald K. Ellis on Black education versus Black freedom

Nicole Eustace on settler colonialism

Agustín Fuentes on human nature

Justene Hill Edwards on the history of inequality in America

Destin Jenkins on a short history of debt

Kelly Lytle Hernández on the immigration regime in America

Natalia Molina on the myth of assimilation

Tony Perry on water in African American culture and history

Beth Piatote on living with history

Ashanté M. Reese on the transformative possibilities of food

Daniel Steinmetz-Jenkins on religion and populism

Onaje X. O. Woodbine on transcendence in sports